D0201345

THE COMPLETE WINESKIN

HAROLD R. EBERLE

The Complete Wineskin (Revised Edition)

© 1993 by Harold R. Eberle

Winepress Publishing
PO Box 10653, Yakima, WA 98909-1653 USA

First Edition: March 1989
Second Edition: April 1990
Third Edition: First Printing, March 1993
                  Second Printing, November 1994
Fourth Edition: First Printing, August 1997
                  Second Printing, June 1998
                  Third Printing, July 1999

Library of Congress Catalog Card No. 92-96961
ISBN 1-882523-02-4

Unless otherwise noted, all biblical quotations are taken from the New American Standard Bible, © 1960, 1962, 1963, 1968, 1971, 1972, 1973, 1975, 1977 by the Lockman Foundation. Used by permission.

Cover by Angela Hopkins

ALL RIGHTS RESERVED
No part of this publication may be reproduced, stored in a retrieval system, or transmitted in any form or by any means—electronic, mechanical, photocopy, recording, or otherwise—without the express prior permission of Winepress Publishing Company, with the exception of brief excerpts in magazine articles and/or reviews.

Printed in the United States of America

All inquiries about reprinting or translating into other languages should be addressed to Winepress Publishing.

THANKS AND DEDICATION

My special thanks go to Annette Bradley, whose God-given experience and generous wisdom have added special graces to this book. Also Barbara and John Milligan, editor and designer respectively, helped and inspired me at critical stages of book production. Pastor David Herr helped me soften key passages in this fourth edition, eliminating many of the negative attitudes evident in my earlier writings. Brian Coontz has demonstrated a Christ-like, servant heart in his willingness to help with graphics work and other computer-related services. And my wife, Linda, is the one who has stood by me through each and every project as we attempt to serve our Lord together.

This book is dedicated to my first born son, Joshua Aaron Eberle.

ABOUT THE AUTHOR

In 1985 Harold R. Eberle left the pastoral ministry to begin traveling throughout the world as a prophetic teacher to the Body of Christ. His words have reached ears in every Christian denomination. He has authored nine books which include: *The Complete Wineskin, The Living Sword, God's Leaders for Tomorrow's World, Two Become One, Accessing the Spiritual World, The Breath of God in Us, Escaping Dualism,* and a two-volume series entitled *Developing a Prosperous Soul.*

Harold founded and heads both Winepress Ministries and Winepress Publishing. With his wife, Linda, and their children, Harold resides in Yakima, Washington, USA.

TABLE OF CONTENTS

Part Four - The Wineskin Now Forming

Epilogue

Introduction

The words of our Lord:

"And no one puts new wine into old wine-skins; otherwise the new wine will burst the skins and it will be spilled out, and the skins will be ruined. But new wine must be put into fresh wineskins" (Luke 5:37-38).

Whenever the Holy Spirit fills people with "new wine," the structure or organization in which they function must change. Old wineskins rip. New wine-skins must be used to hold the additional life and power of God.

We have seen this principle in operation throughout the history of the Church. When Martin Luther received revelation from the Holy Spirit concerning faith and grace, the established church in that day was ripped in two and a new denomination under Luther was born. When John Wesley preached with the fire of the Spirit, a new structure, now known as the Methodist denomination, had to be formed. The same process has occurred again and again as great men or women ministered under a fresh anointing of God's Spirit. And, of course, we have seen how thousands of churches have formed over the last fifty years as members received a baptism of the Holy Spirit with various manifestations. A new wineskin formed each time new wine was poured in.

God is pouring new wine into us. Christians all over the world have been crying out to God for a fresh outpouring of His Spirit. Our Lord has never failed His Church. Repeatedly, He has brought powerful spiritual awakenings. Many believe that the last outpouring of God's Spirit that is promised in the Bible (Joel 2:28-29) will soon take place. The time for God to move is at hand.

Therefore, we should expect our present wineskins to rip. Jesus taught that it is impossible to pour new wine into an old wineskin without ripping it. There can be no mighty spiritual awakening in our day without a great shaking of our Church organizations, leaders, and structures. If you are looking for the Second Coming of Jesus, or if you are praying to God to move upon your church, your city, your local schools, your family, or your own heart, then the first thing you must look for is a new wineskin.

How will the present wineskin of the Church be changed? We cannot expect to know the same power of the Holy Spirit that the New Testament believers experienced unless we have wineskins similar to theirs. One of the major changes will have to do with the full operation of what we call the five ministry gifts: apostle, prophet, evangelist, pastor, and teacher (Eph. 4:11).

Many Christians have thought that the apostle and prophet were only for New Testament times, but that is wrong. Ephesians 4:11-13 tells us that all five of these gifts were given by God to the Church "until we all attain to the unity of the faith, and of the knowledge of the Son of God, to a mature man, to the measure of the stature which belongs to the fulness of Christ." The Church will never reach its fulness nor any form of unity until all five ministry gifts are functioning together in the Body of Christ.

Today, God is raising up leaders who have these gifts. The Church is now undergoing a major reformation in its structure that will enable it to handle a great outpouring of God's Spirit.

This is the reason I have written this book. I want to share with you some of the ways the present organization of the Church is ripping and the new wineskin is being formed. We will look first at the ministry gifts and at other leadership positions in the church, and then at how the leaders in those positions are to work in unity and power.

Throughout the book I have used the capitalized word Church to refer to the whole Body of Christ, which is made up of all those throughout the world who believe in Jesus. The word church, with lower case "c," will refer to any local group of Christians who gather regularly for prayer, fellowship, worship, and teaching.

Part One

An
Overview
of the
Ministry Gifts

CHAPTER 1

THE PURPOSES OF
THE MINISTRY GIFTS

And He gave some as apostles, and some
as prophets, and some as evangelists,
and some as pastors and teachers, for the
equipping of the saints for the work of
service, to the building up of the body of
Christ (Eph. 4:11-12).

We refer to the five gifts named in these verses as
ministry gifts. They are ministries, or callings, that
God has ordained to equip and lead His Church.

We must not confuse the ministry gifts with other
gifts mentioned in the Bible. All Christians may have
gifts such as tongues, healing, words of knowledge,
giving, and so on; these gifts are for serving within the
Body of Christ. In contrast, the five ministry gifts are
callings for the oversight of the Church.

Nor should we confuse the ministry gifts with the
ongoing *ministries* that every born-again Christian
has. For example, every believer should be involved
in evangelism, but only a few have the gift of evangelist. In the same way, all believers should exhort,
teach, and care for one another, but not all have a
calling as a pastor or teacher. Paul tells us that all

Christians should desire to prophesy (I Cor. 14:1), but this does not mean that all are called as prophets. Even apostolic work, which will be described later, should be done to some extent by every believer, but few have the ministry gift of apostle. The gifts of teacher, pastor, evangelist, prophet, and apostle are leadership positions from which we should all learn so that we ourselves can be involved to a lesser degree in the ministries of teaching, pastoring, evangelizing, and so on.

The unique characteristic of a ministry gift is the anointing of God. The word *anointed* means "having oil spread upon." A person becomes anointed by experiencing God's Spirit coming upon, and transforming, him or her in a special way.

In the Old Testament it is especially clear through numerous examples that men and women dramatically changed when they became anointed by God. Just before Saul is anointed, Samuel says to him, "'Then the Spirit of the LORD will come upon you mightily, and you shall...be changed into another man'" (1 Sam. 10:6).

The moment a person becomes anointed, a transformation takes place. Every leader with a ministry gift has been touched, or gifted, by God, and hence changed by the work of the Spirit. These changes take place in two areas of a person's life. First, a gift from God changes the person's heart. The Bible tells us that the instant Saul received his anointing "God changed his heart" (1 Sam. 10:9). So also a pastor receives a heart to shepherd people, and an evangelist receives a heart full of compassion for the lost. It is God's own heart for a specific area of ministry that is placed within the gifted individual.

8

Second, a gift from God also allows the Holy Spirit to flow through a person in greater measure and in a certain fashion. Jesus explained that the Holy Spirit flows out of believers like rivers of living water from their innermost being (John 7:38-39). The Spirit will work through any Christian, but the person who has received God's heart for a ministry has an open channel for the Spirit to flow in a unique way. The Spirit comes forth from the pastor in a different manner than the way He works through the teacher. It is the same Spirit, sent by God the Father, but the different gifts allow God to pour out His grace in different ways.

As the Holy Spirit flows through an individual, those who are receiving the Holy Spirit's ministry are set free in various areas of their lives. Isaiah tells us that the anointing of God breaks the yoke (Is. 10:27 KJV). The anointing of a pastor allows the Holy Spirit to flow to other people and break certain yokes and bondages that have held them captive. Likewise, an evangelist can break other kinds of bondages and bring freedom to people.

As the anointing flows through an individual's heart, it breaks bondages off of others' lives.

This anointing — which transforms a person's heart, creates a channel through which the Holy Spirit can flow, and releases power to break yokes of bondage — is what we need to consider as we study each of the five ministry gifts.

CHAPTER 2

PASTORS, TEACHERS, AND EVANGELISTS

Rather than discuss the five ministry gifts in the order given in Ephesians 4:11-12, we will look first at the three that are the most familiar to Christians: pastors, teachers, and evangelists. Be prepared, however, to lay aside your assumptions about all five ministry gifts as we look at each one in detail.

PASTORS

When we say "pastor," we tend to think of the visible leader who runs a church, preaches two or three times a week, and counsels people in need. But we need to change our concept of what a pastor is. *The gift of pastor is an anointing from God — a gift that transforms the recipient's heart and allows the Holy Spirit to break certain bondages.* We must focus on these aspects. The heart of a pastor is to care for and shepherd people. True pastors hurt when their people have difficulties, and rejoice when their people are joyfully walking with God. The eyes and thoughts of pastors are continually on their flocks. The lives of pastors become intimately involved with their congregations. The gift that pastors possess is nothing less than the heart of God to shepherd His people.

The anointing of pastors allows the Holy Spirit to flow through them in a way that causes people to be supernaturally drawn together. The pastoral anointing breaks bondages off people — bondages that cause them to be independent, isolated, and insecure. The Holy Spirit-guided words that come out of the hearts and mouths of pastors make their listeners able to relax, come together, and feel secure in the Body of Christ. It is common to hear a true pastor say things like, "I'm glad you're here," "How's your family?," "Is there anything I can do for you?," and other disarming phrases that express personal concern. Pastors are God's channels through whom God shelters His people and shows His intimate love. Pastors are shepherds, anointed to gather God's flock out of the world.

We need to realize that many Christian leaders today who are called pastors do not have God's anointing to pastor. When I began in ministry, I was put in charge of a church, and my entire congregation called me the pastor. But I did not have a heart for the people that a true pastor has. I enjoyed teaching, and I gave fairly good sermons on Sunday mornings, but people were not supernaturally drawn to me for counsel and love. I can remember the very day, after about six months in that position, when God gave me the gift of pastor. I spent an evening burdened with the needs of the congregation and crying to God to help them. That night, my heart changed, and they became "my people." From then on, they had a supernatural trust in me, and a spiritual bond was formed between us.

As I travel, I meet ministers who have never received the gift of pastor. A few look at the position as a job, but they are what the Bible calls "hirelings" (John 10:12-13), for they are not bound spiritually to the people. Other ministers are sincere in serving God, and they may be successful, but their success is due to their teaching, preaching, and/or administrative skills instead of to the pastoral anointing. And then there are churches in which the person anointed to pastor does not have the title of pastor but instead serves as an elder, deacon, Sunday school teacher, or Bible study leader. Unfortunately, our natural titles do not always match the God-given anointings.

In many churches, several congregational members have an anointing to pastor, but that anointing may be for a ministry to a specific group within the church. A person with a heart for children may be a children's pastor; to that person, the children will be supernaturally drawn. I know of a man whose heart and ministry are directed toward the elderly, and he serves as a pastor to them under the senior minister. Some youth workers are simply leaders or teachers, but other youth workers are anointed by God as youth pastors. Pastoral anointings may be on several people in one congregation.

No denomination, board, or individual can give anyone the gift of pastoring. Human beings can recognize, but cannot produce, God's gifts. A pastor is not someone with a seminary education or a denominational certificate. A pastor is a Christian leader who has a certain anointing: the gift of God's heart to shepherd people and to draw them together out of the world and into the Body of Christ. This gift comes only from God.

TEACHERS

The gift of teacher is an anointing from God that stirs a person to help others understand God's truths. Teachers have hearts for people, and it troubles them to see others in bondage due to misunderstanding God's principles. The Sunday school teacher who is earnestly concerned that the children learn Bible truths has God's gift of teaching, whereas the Sunday school teacher who serves only out of duty does not have this anointing. A congregational member willing to sacrifice much time and energy to teach a Bible study is the one whom God has anointed. Teachers are not identified by their education or Bible knowledge, but rather by their hearts. Nor can they be known by their skill at teaching, for there is also a natural talent of teaching, which has nothing to do with God's heart. Just as there are hirelings who are wrongly called pastors, so also are there naturally skilled teachers in our Bible schools, seminaries, and churches. It is only those who are burdened with the needs of people, and hence motivated from their hearts to teach, that are called and anointed by God.

Only those with such a heart have the Holy Spirit's power flowing through their teaching. The anointing breaks yokes off the listeners, freeing them from Satan's lies and the world's deceptions. Anointed teachers are not those who just teach doctrines or impart knowledge, but they are individuals who, by explaining God's truths, set people free of sin, natural limitations, depression, fear, anxiety, and other bondages. A naturally gifted teacher may be able to explain to a person why that person sins and what the Bible has to say about the sin, but a teacher who is spiritually gifted releases power through that gift to set the other person free. The Spirit of truth (John 14:17), who sets people free (John 8:32), works with and through the Spirit-anointed teacher.

EVANGELISTS

The word *evangelist* means in Greek "one who announces good tidings." An evangelist is not as greatly concerned about imparting deep spiritual truths as the teacher is, but is motivated to help people understand and respond to the basic biblical messages. The evangelist's primary concern is to help non-Christians find salvation and the forgiveness of sins. The cry of the evangelist's heart toward other Christians is to motivate them to respond to basic mandates such as "Go into all the world and preach the gospel..." (Mark 16:15). The evangelist is a proclaimer of the fundamental Christian beliefs.

The Holy Spirit works with the evangelist to motivate the listeners. Through the anointing that is on the evangelist, people are emotionally stirred and crowds are easily attracted. The Holy Spirit flows out in a way that convicts people of their sins. Excuses for inactivity and indecisiveness are exposed by the light of the Spirit. All listeners are spiritually urged to respond and act.

The evangelist is usually an aggressive, energetic person. In order to motivate others to act, the evangelist must be an active individual who enjoys seeing quick results, big crowds, and fast change. The anointed evangelist is constantly moving and is exciting to be around.

15

Evangelists can be found both inside and outside the local church. In the book of Acts we see Philip, who is called an evangelist (21:8), preaching the Gospel in one city after another (8:40); Philip was also used by God to share the Gospel one-on-one with unbelievers (8:29-38). In his own church he was one of the seven deacons who waited on tables (6:1-5). Some evangelists preach to Christians, while others are sent out to minister to the world.

CHAPTER 3

DO WE HAVE
EARS TO HEAR?

Before we discuss prophets and apostles, let's think about our own receptivity to these gifts. Most of us are not familiar with these ministries, and therefore, we must be careful to understand them.

Jesus talked about "ears to hear" (Mark 4:9, for example). Even His disciples were not yet ready to hear certain truths. A person's rejection of truth is not usually an open denial, but rather a subtle acceptance of one's own thoughts instead of God's. For example, millions have rejected the "born again" experience by holding to their own thoughts, such as, *It's not for me,* or *I'm not ready,* or *Maybe before I die.* Those thoughts assign the "born again" experience to someone else or to a different time. People with those thoughts hold the truth at arm's length so that they feel no obligation to respond.

Clinging to thoughts that keep the truth away from us makes us unable to hear. This is what it means to be hard-hearted. Many Christians are hard-hearted toward the Holy Spirit's gift of tongues. They reason that this gift is for only a select few, or that tongues passed away long ago, or that it is only for a few missionaries overseas. They harden their hearts so that they are unwilling to respond personally, and instead assign the gift of tongues to other people, other times, or distant places.

The same is true with the issue of physical healing. Many Christians hope that God will take away their sicknesses someday in the future. Others deny supernatural healing altogether in this age, while most recognize that it may happen to another person, but to receive it themselves is an entirely different matter. Jesus knew that the centurion was ready to have his servant healed when the centurion said to Jesus, "'...Just say the word, and my servant will be healed'" (Matt. 8:8). When we say, "Right now it will happen," then our hearts are open and we are ready to receive. Then we have hearing ears.

This principle is no different with the gifts of prophet and apostle. For years the Church has dismissed such gifts, saying they were for the New Testament times or just for the twelve original apostles plus a few people in the Old Testament. Much of the Church has been unable to accept the fact that at least 22 apostles are named in the New Testament (we'll list these later) and that prophets are mentioned over 150 times. To admit that apostles and prophets are here today in our midst is another leap of faith, which requires hearing ears. We tend to reject truths that we do not want to hear. Such is the case with prophets and apostles, because for us to recognize them as part of today's Church means we will have to reorganize our church structure and change our personal lives. However, we will not have ears to understand these gifts until we acknowledge that all five ministry gifts are for us today — *now*.

We each need to ask ourselves, Do I have ears to hear? Am I still pushing prophets and apostles off to another time or place? Could I accept someone in my city, church, or family who claims to be an apostle? Am I willing to admit that I am a prophet (if that is what you now realize)? Am I ready to say, "Today is the day!"?

It is not enough to accept apostles as leaders who are in foreign countries on the mission field. Remember, every country is a mission field. Every nation *needs* apostles and prophets.

We cannot just point at our great Christian leaders who have large television, radio, and magazine ministries, and call *them* our apostles and prophets, for that attitude also is a form of hardening our hearts and moving them away from us personally. We accept God's gifts when we look for them right in our midst — in our own lives and in our own churches.

As we accept prophets and apostles, we receive their ministries, and thereby open up tremendous channels of God's power into the Church and into the world. We see in the Bible that it was the prophets and the apostles who had the greatest authority, often demonstrated by miracles and healings. As the pastors, teachers, and evangelists have specific anointings that allow the rivers of life to flow, so also do the prophets and apostles. In fact, as we will see, prophets and apostles have a greater flow of grace than any of the others. Because the Church, to only a limited degree, has accepted all five ministry gifts, it has not experienced the fullness of God's power. If you have been praying for God's power to be brought to the Church, then get ready to receive all the vessels through which it will come.

Finally, it is not enough just to acknowledge that prophets and apostles do exist, but we must accept them and their anointings. Let me apply this acceptance to the baptism of the Holy Spirit. It is not enough for a person to recognize that such an experience is true or possible. Only one who *accepts* the baptism will enjoy the related benefits. In the same way, those who only admit to the existence of prophets and apostles, but do not accept them, will not benefit from their anointings. Jesus said that if you receive a prophet, you receive Jesus Himself (Matt. 10:40-41). It is time we receive the prophets and apostles.

CHAPTER 4

FOUNDATION WORKERS: PROPHETS AND APOSTLES

A unique characteristic of the prophetic and apostolic anointings is that they work on the basic structure of the Church. Ephesians 2:20 tells us about the Body of Christ, which is "built upon the foundation of the apostles and prophets, Christ Jesus Himself being the corner stone."

Evangelists, pastors, teachers, and all other Christians build upon the foundation already laid (see also 1 Cor. 3:10-13). Only apostles and prophets have the empowering of God to lay or change the foundation itself. This will become evident as we look at these two gifts individually.

PROPHETS

The word *prophet* means "one who speaks forth." A prophet is a Christian who God calls to speak out for Him, not in the usual way that a preacher expounds or teaches from the Bible, but in a much more direct and powerful way. Behind a prophet's words are great spiritual forces, able to break spiritual bondages off individuals or groups of people. As God's words at

Creation — such as "Let there be light" — held creative power, so also a prophet's words, to a lesser degree, carry God's creative power. The purpose of the prophet's words is not simply to provide knowledge or understanding, but to change the structure or nature of that which is being spoken to. A preacher's words may be evaluated, but a prophet's words must be accepted or rejected, submitted to or resisted. This does not mean that the ongoing conversation of a prophet is God-ordained, and hence power-packed, but the messages that the prophet receives from God for a particular situation or person do have God's spiritual forces behind them. The prophet is God's direct mouthpiece, through whom God speaks powerfully into the church and into the world.

We must distinguish between the Christian who prophesies and the ministry gift of a prophet. As I implied earlier, confusing these two is as wrong as equating a Christian who does evangelistic work with the Christian who has the gift of evangelist. The Christian who prophesies speaks God's words, but there is not as much spiritual power behind those words, and they are spoken only for edification, consolation, and exhortation (1 Cor. 14:3). The prophet may speak with these three purposes, but also may speak God's direction, revelation, rebuke, correction, or knowledge of the future. The prophets in Acts 13:1-2 hear God's direction to send out Paul and Barnabas for ministry. In Acts 21:10-11 the prophet Agabus speaks with revelation and knowledge of the future when he announces that Paul will be imprisoned. The prophets in the Old Testament give strong rebukes to the Jewish people on many occasions, as does Paul in his letters to the churches. The ministry of a prophet is more diversified and powerful than that of a Christian who simply prophesies.

The prophet can be better understood when we contrast the power of the prophet's words with that of an evangelist's words. A gifted evangelist may come to a church or a city and preach a message that causes dozens or even hundreds of people to respond. However, we know from studies that success depends much upon advertising, organization, and extensive follow-up — and even with these, very few of the people reached will remain involved in a church. For example, in a typical citywide evangelistic crusade held today, less than twenty percent of those who respond to the Gospel invitation will get involved in a church.

In contrast, when a prophet visits a church or a city, the power of the prophet's words produces lasting results. Charles Finney (who is wrongly called an evangelist by many) was a prophet who brought revival to numerous cities in America about one hundred years ago. Studies show that over eighty percent of those to whom he ministered remained in churches for the rest of their lives. The prophet Jonah brought an entire city to repentance without any advertising, follow-up, or administration.

Such results are understandable in the prophet's ministry but uncommon in the ministry of the evangelist. A gifted prophet not only changes the course of a church for years to come, but individuals who receive the prophet's ministry are given direction that influences the rest of their lives. The prophet deals with foundations. As we look at a few other examples later, we will see that a prophet's words endure time, persecution, and affliction. The words of teachers, pastors, and evangelists do not carry such authority.

Often the prophet is called upon by God for a specific task. John the Baptist was sent to prepare the way for the Lord. Nehemiah led the Jews to rebuild the wall around Jerusalem. When we read the books of the prophets in the Bible, we see that "the word of the Lord" or a vision came to each of them and then they were required to proclaim that one message. Moses, who was also a prophet, led the Hebrew people out of captivity.

Today, God sends some prophets to a specific church or denomination to correct it or to help get it on track. Other prophets may have a primary message that they express in many different ways and carry to many churches. Because of this, they may appear unbalanced and limited. People may judge them for talking about the same topics over and over, not realizing that they are *supposed* to be "unbalanced," at least through our natural eyes. Many times God will keep the prophet speaking on the same subject or on related topics until the message has been received or openly rejected. After that, the prophet may be given a new vision, or word, or burden from God. It is because the prophet's mission can be intense and powerful that the prophet is sometimes limited to one task or message at a time.

We must not form a distorted image of the prophet's ministry. Not all prophets have a single mission or purpose. Most of them should be able to give consistent, balanced direction and revelation within the Body. In describing their role, I do not want to restrict them or your view of what they should do. I am just briefly mentioning here a few common characteristics.

Prophets are also used by God to transmit, confirm, or recognize anointings on other people. In the Old Testament, we see that the prophets poured oil on the heads of the kings before the kings took their positions. Paul encourages Timothy to continue in the spiritual gifting he received through the laying on of hands with prophetic utterance (1 Tim. 1:18 and 4:14). It was several prophets and teachers that set Paul and Barnabas aside for ministry (Acts 13:1-3). Prophets are able to speak forth God's anointings as God directs.

The hearts of prophets are directed, intense, burdened, tender, and sometimes frustrated. Their hearts are focused on the specific tasks God has given them. Their emotions are linked to the results they perceive in relationship to their calling. They are often in tears when they see no change, joyful when correction is received. They have tender hearts that are easily broken at the sight of sin. Yet, it is common for prophets to be frustrated when they see that what is written in the Bible is not real in the Church.

Prophets are more sensitive to spiritual forces and impending troubles than the average Christian. In the Old Testament, prophets are often called *seers*, referring to their ability to see into the spiritual world (for example, 1 Samuel 9:9). They sense God's solutions or answers to problems in the Church, in the world, and in the lives of individuals. Their eyes are open to see visions and anointings from God.

Because prophets often encounter tremendous resistance, many of them are very determined, assertive people, frequently considered hardheaded and stubborn. They are not influenced much by persecution or men's opinions. They are often dramatic, acting in ways that emphasize the messages God has placed on their hearts. Prophets are sometimes radical individuals, alone more than the average Christian, and so intense that they challenge those around them. I do not want to stereotype, but this is how God very often seems to design the character and personality of a prophet. It comes with the gift.

APOSTLES

The word *apostle* means in Greek "one sent forth." A true apostle is a minister *sent by God to accomplish a specific work.* Note that an apostle is not sent by an organization, a church, or a group of people.

The twelve men who walked with Jesus were called apostles from the day Jesus sent them out to the cities to preach about the Kingdom of God; before that time, they were called disciples. In Acts 13 we see that Paul and Barnabas become apostles at the time that the Holy Spirit separates them to go out and preach. Paul begins his letter to the Galatians with his personal qualifications: "Paul an apostle (not sent from men, nor through the agency of man, but through Jesus Christ, and God the Father, who raised Him from the dead)..." (Gal. 1:1).

Apostles may have a denomination, a church, or a certain group behind them, but they always have a higher call from God. The first identifying mark of apostles is that they are indeed "sent ones."

The second identifying mark of apostles is their spiritual authority. Paul defends his own position as an apostle by writing, "The signs of a true apostle were performed among you with all perseverance, by signs and wonders and miracles" (2 Cor. 12:12). We see Paul demonstrating great authority when God uses him to perform miracles and when he delivers a sinful man over to Satan (1 Cor. 5:1-5). An apostle can also release blessings through his words, prayers, and the laying on of hands.

The word *missionary* has the same root as *apostle*: both mean "one sent forth." However, today's missionaries are true apostles only if they have been sent specifically by God and if apostolic authority is operating in their ministries. Some missionaries have been sent out overseas, and indeed they have functioned as apostles to certain countries or regions. However, not all missionaries are apostles, and not all apostles are sent to strange lands.

The apostolic gift includes the ability to do whatever is necessary to accomplish what God has sent the apostle to do. Apostles have grace to minister in the other four ministry gifts: prophet, evangelist, pastor, and teacher. Just as pastors have supernatural drawing power for their flocks, apostles also attract leaders with the gifts of pastor, teacher, evangelists, and prophet. Each apostle normally raises up several pastors, evangelists, teachers, and other leaders to help fulfill the calling that God has given to the apostle.

The calling of an apostle is specific to a region or a people. Paul writes that he is *an apostle to the Gentiles* and that Peter is *an apostle to the Jews* (Gal. 2:8). To be sent by God implies that one is sent to a place or to a group of people. We have leaders who have been used as apostles to Africa or China or certain cities. Some apostles may minister to smaller groups of people, such as the Laotian refugees in Chicago or the homeless in Los Angeles. Others may be sent by God to build a foundation for a specific ministry within the Body of Christ. We will look at examples of all these later.

Apostles are different from prophets, though they all have specific tasks. Prophets have limited messages or purposes, and the power of prophets is in their words. Apostles are sent forth to establish and build up groups of believers in all areas of the believers' lives. Apostles become *fathers* to their ministries, and they may remain as heads of those ministries, each apostle overseeing several leaders, or they may move on, as Paul did, handing over the established work to someone else. The ministries of apostles are inclusive and broader than those of prophets. Furthermore, the foundations that endure are not their words but their works.

The hearts of apostles are tied into every area of what they are called to do. They see the overall ministry. They are burdened for the churches, the leaders, and all the people under their care. Paul wrote that he was constantly under a pressure of concern for all the churches (2 Cor. 11:28).

Apostles supernaturally know when a part of their work needs help or when a minister under their care is suffering. The hearts of apostles are *big*. Out of their big hearts flow a spiritual blessing and an anointing for those under them. Pastors, teachers, evangelists, and the entire ministries under apostles are supernaturally empowered and protected by the Holy Spirit. This is the reason Paul could release a sinful man to Satan by withdrawing God's protective hand (2 Cor. 5:5). When an apostle is present, unity and peace flow into the organization. Those who function under an apostle receive through that apostle the Holy Spirit's energy, zeal, and anointing. This is the way that the Holy Spirit flows from the apostle's innermost being.

Again, let's remember that at least twenty-two people in the New Testament are called apostles. Besides the original twelve, they are Matthias (Acts 1:26); Barnabas and Paul (Acts 14:14); Andronicus and Junius (Rom. 16:7); James the Lord's brother (Gal. 1:19); Epaphroditus (Phil. 2:25); Apollos (1 Cor. 4:6-9); and Silvanus and Timothy (1 Thess. 1:1, 2:6). Some Scriptures imply that even more were considered apostles (for example, see Rom. 16:7).

Of course, these twenty-two or more apostles were overseeing the Church when the number of believers was a fraction of what it is today. We should expect many more apostles to oversee the present-day Church worldwide. Since Ephesians 4:11-12 tells us that the apostles are needed for the building up of the Body until we all attain to the unity of the faith, then we should be able to recognize more than the original twelve apostles. We should recognize dozens, if not hundreds, of leaders who have served as apostles throughout the history of the Church.

EXAMPLES OF APOSTLES AND PROPHETS

In order to better understand the prophetic and apostolic positions, let's look at some examples of well-known Christian leaders who have functioned in these anointings. By mentioning these, I am not implying that I agree with everything they teach or for which they stand, so please do not let your feelings about any of them keep you from seeing their ministries as examples.

One of the most well-known prophets was Martin Luther. We could consider his life and see that he moved into the prophetic office when he brought forth a bold message emphasizing salvation through faith and the priesthood of all believers. He encountered incredible persecution and yet firmly held to the word of the Lord, which he was sent to proclaim. As his message became established and accepted, thousands of Christians followed him. Then he moved into a more apostolic ministry. He became the father of the Lutheran denomination, with many ministers under him helping to fulfill the vision God had given him.

John Wesley also could be considered a prophet. He boldly preached the Holy Spirit's work of witnessing salvation in men's hearts and then making them holy to God. Very few leaders accepted Wesley at first, yet his words shook the Christian world. In order to sustain his work, God later placed an apostolic anointing upon him, which enabled him to organize and lead a movement that became known as the Methodist denomination.

Several men and women of God have been sent prophetically to the world to bring the message of divine healing. John Alexander Dowie, Aimee Semple McPherson, Kathryn Kuhlmann, and Oral Roberts all preached of the power and love of God to heal the sick. At first their messages were not accepted by the Church. However, in time the power of their words stood while the Church had to yield. Such are the words of a prophet. Oral Roberts and Aimee Semple McPherson later moved into apostolic positions from which their ministries would be maintained and leaders would be raised up to carry on with the visions from God.

Evan Roberts, Leonard Ravenhill, Charles Finney, and Frank Bartelmann, along with several others, have been used by God as prophets to bring messages concerning revival.

David Wilkerson is an excellent example of a man whom God has used in several ministry gifts. While pastoring a small church, he received a vision from God to reach the street youth in the big cities of America. With this apostolic calling, he left his church and went to the cities. Out of that ministry a network of outreaches known as Teen Challenge sprang up. Since then, God has moved Wilkerson back into a prophetic office with a word to the Church to repent and to get holy before God. Wilkerson continues to function in both the apostolic and the prophetic ministries.

Many parachurch organizations have been directed by people with apostolic anointings. Each of these people has been give a specific work that has never been done before. Bill Bright is the head of Campus Crusade for Christ. Loren Cunningham is the apostle to thousands involved in Youth With A Mission. Demos Shakarian had a call from God to start The Full Gospel Business Men's Fellowship. If we were to study Inter Varsity Christian Fellowship, Youth for Christ, The Navigators, Maranatha Ministries, and other ministries, we would be able to identify a great many other leaders with apostolic anointings.

Other individuals are worth mentioning here. Keith Green was used as a prophet to correct much compromising that was going on in the Church. Smith Wigglesworth and Kenneth Hagin have spoken as prophets with messages of faith, but Hagin moved into an apostolic ministry when he started his Bible Training Center and began sending out Christian leaders throughout the world. Bob Mumford and others made the Church aware of the need for discipleship. Dr. David Yonggi Cho has prophetically brought a message on church growth, but he also, like so many others with a prophetic message, moved into an apostolic ministry. Hudson Taylor was an apostle to China, as John G. Lake was to South Africa. John Wimber served as an apostle over the Vineyard churches. Hundreds of other Christian leaders — including some who have been used in individual cities or churches — are gifted as apostles and/or prophets. They are simply less well known.

Forgive me if I have left out your favorite man or woman of God. We need to recognize that God has many, many prophets and apostles scattered throughout the history of the Church and throughout the world today. We may not agree with everything that each of these leaders teaches, but their prophetic and apostolic influence upon the Body of Christ cannot be denied. They all have lain a foundation on which Christians will be building for years to come, and that fact establishes them as true apostles and prophets.

CHAPTER 5

VARYING GIFTS

A leader is not necessarily locked into one gift. Some of the examples we have just examined show how ministers can grow and move into greater anointings. A leader also may experience various gifts in a relatively short period of time. The leader may be used as an apostle when speaking to certain people and as a pastor when ministering to others. The Holy Spirit can flow through a speaker in a prophetic anointing one time and in a teaching anointing at a later time. Many preachers have experienced such changes.

A leader's anointing is determined to a great extent by the needs and hunger of the people. Those receiving ministry draw spiritual strength from the leader. The more eager they are to receive God's wisdom, direction, and power, the more they "pull" on the minister, thereby releasing the Holy Spirit to move. If they need a prophetic voice, the anointing upon a teacher may be altered in that direction. A pastor may be turned into an evangelist or even an apostle when going overseas and preaching to the masses. The Holy Spirit, who knows the needs of the people, ministers as He sees fit and as He is allowed to flow.

Many people who have received callings from God to function in certain anointings have rejected those callings. Just as Jonah refused for a time to answer God's bidding, so also many Christians today have not yielded to the ministries God has offered them. Some are ministers who have settled for second best. Others are among the laity sitting in church pews Sunday after Sunday, unsure of how to respond. And then some are running from God even to the extent of avoiding all contact with the Christian community. (I am convinced that many of those called by God are hiding in bars or are engrossed in careers that consume their every thought.) The willingness of a person's heart is pivotal in the release of God's Spirit flowing through that person.

Another factor in determining the Spirit's flow is the spiritual condition of the minister. I have found that the more I have prayed and built up myself spiritually before a service, the more likely I will be used in a higher anointing. As will be explained later, the apostolic and prophetic gifts are *higher* than the evangelistic, pastoral, or teaching anointings. Whenever our hearts are full of faith, the channel of power is open for the greater flow of the Holy Spirit.

Of course, an individual usually functions under the same anointing for a long time. This is partly because a leader typically ministers to the same group of people for an extended period. Also, God requires each of us to go through a "growing" time, and He does not move most of us too quickly from one ministry to another. Most Christian leaders each function with one ministry gift for many years.

CHAPTER 6

CONFUSION IN THE CHURCH

It is time that we clear up the confusion in our Church leadership. It is obvious that our modern titles and positions do not correspond very well to God's anointings. Many individuals today are being called pastors when they are actually anointed as teachers or evangelists. Some are called pastors by people or denominations, even though God would prefer to recognize them as prophets or apostles. Others are naturally talented as businesspeople, and they have no calling to the church ministry. Still other ministry gifts are hidden behind the title of superintendent, bishop, youth leader, assistant pastor, board president, Bible study leader, trustee, and so on. The Church has developed titles through traditions instead of by the Word of God. Many of them are natural positions, much like those in a large business or corporation. These titles may not be evil or wrong, but the Church always will be in confusion until we correlate a leader's anointing with his or her title.

There are several reasons why we must pay closer attention to the individual anointings of God:

1) In the New Testament, we do not see Christian leaders being labeled as president, assistant pastor or superintendent or anything else short of their gifts.

A prophet is called a prophet. Philip is recognized as an evangelist. We want our churches to be biblical, and, therefore, our titles ought to be biblical.

2) When Christians recognize their own anointings, they move more fully into those anointings.

Suppose you have the gift of pastor. As soon as you recognize supernatural power flowing through you that causes other people to follow you, you step out even more boldly to use your God-given authority. In contrast, if you are a youth leader who thinks you have only natural strength and wisdom, you will not have much confidence that God is working with you. Prophets who accept the fact that they are anointed by God will speak out with more authority than will superintendents. Apostles can unashamedly give leadership and direction to many pastors when they know that God has called them as apostles. *Naming* an anointing is essential for understanding that anointing and for functioning in it freely with God's power.

3) Others, too, need to recognize a leader's anointing.

If you do not look to your pastor as your pastor, you will not receive as much from that pastor. Until you recognize the gifting and calling of God on your pastor's life, you will have certain reservations and even some skepticism that can hinder the Holy Spirit from flowing to you freely. In the same way, prophets who are not received as prophets cannot minister fully in their anointings. Our Lord said that if we receive a prophet in the name of a prophet, we receive Jesus (Matt. 10:40-41). Even He was unable to function as a prophet in His home town, because they would not accept Him (Mark 6:1-6). If we do not recognize someone's anointing, we limit the flow of God's power through that person. If, however, we receive the anointed person's ministry, we receive Jesus.

4) We must recognize the anointings of our leaders so that we will know what to expect from them.

Since today's Church has classified most of its leaders as pastors, we tend to expect all of them to act in caring, personal, pastoral ways. But such limited thinking hinders the other gifts from operating. When a Christian goes to a prophet, that Christian should expect to receive a different kind of ministry than what he or she would receive from a pastor. Perhaps the prophet will give a word from the Lord, a rebuke, or a revelation, rather than counseling. Likewise, an evangelist ministers differently than a teacher ministers. Unless we start calling our leaders by their God-given anointings, we will not understand how God desires to work through them.

5) Christians who are functioning outside their anointings cannot live the victorious, Spirit-filled life.

Romans 12:6 tells us, "And since we have gifts that differ according to the grace given to us, let each exercise them accordingly...." Within the gifts we have received, we have grace. Those who try to function outside their anointings will not have the same supernatural flow of life. The pastor who tries to function as a prophet moves into natural strength. The evangelist who attempts to pastor restricts the flow of the Holy Spirit, which often leads to defeat in many areas. Just this year I have watched two of the most anointed evangelists I know try to pastor churches. Both failed. Often ministers functioning outside their anointings "burn out" and end up frustrated and sometimes angry at God and at the Church. Other ministers who move outside their areas of anointing get involved in sin, finding themselves unable to resist temptations that would not influence them if they were in their areas of grace. It is vital for all ministers to know their anointings so that they can stay in those anointings and thereby benefit from God's grace to live in victory.

6) If we do not recognize various ministry gifts, we will never have all five in operation.

A congregation that is content to have a pastor, an assistant pastor, trustees, and three Sunday school teachers will not have apostles, prophets, and evangelists. If we focus on natural titles, we too easily miss God's plan for leadership in the Church, and then we substitute our system for His.

7) We must recognize anointings because Holy Spirit power requires Holy Spirit words.

As Paul explains, if we desire to function in true spiritual power, we must combine spiritual thoughts with spiritual words (1 Cor. 2:13). The more a church operates in *natural* power, the easier it is to use natural titles the way a corporation or secular club does. The fact that a church adequately can describe its leadership in titles like assistant pastor, trustee, counselor, executive member, and so on, should send a warning signal to you. The church has not needed to understand apostles, prophets, or evangelists, because it has not seen the full power that comes through their anointings. This is the day in which Christians are beginning to recognize all five ministry gifts. The wineskin of the New Testament is becoming the wineskin of our age. The Holy Spirit power that is about to be released into the Body of Christ can be understood only in the language of the Holy Spirit. And His words are based on His anointings.

Now let's go on to discover the wineskin, that is the structure, of the New Testament Church.

Part Two

The
New Testament
Wineskin

CHAPTER 7

LEARNING TO THINK ANEW

In the next few chapters we discover the wineskin, that is the structure, of the New Testament Church. As we look at the organization, the positions, the anointings, the leaders of the local church, and the interactions among those leaders, we must set aside our preconceived ideas on these topics so that we can see the truth clearly. All of us have certain concepts about how the local church should be run. Some of these ideas we have learned by studying the Bible, but others have been assimilated through our own experiences of the present-day church. Without realizing it, we have developed certain ways of thinking that hinder us from accepting different ideas, even if the new ideas are more biblically accurate.

Let me challenge a commonly accepted idea deeply rooted in the minds of most Protestant churchgoers. A typical North American Christian who visits a church today tries immediately to find out who the pastor is. The accepted pattern of organization for the local church is to have a pastor at the head, with the congregation involved under him in varying degrees. However, this pattern is foreign to the New Testament. Nowhere in the Bible can we find a "pastor" leading a congregation. In fact the word *pastor* is used as a noun only once in the entire New Testament, and that is in Ephesians 4:11, where the five ministry gifts are listed. In that passage we are shown that the pastor is part of a team for the equipping of the saints; the pastor is not the head of that team, but is placed fourth in the listing. Where, then, did most of us get our understanding of what a pastor is? From the Bible? I challenge that idea because there is not a single person called a pastor in the New Testament. In contrast, there are twenty-two apostles and many prophets.

Our preconceived ideas too easily cloud our understanding of the Bible. Since most Christians think of a pastor as the person who runs the local church, they have a difficult time recognizing any other organizational structure in the New Testament. For example, in Acts 15 we see many elders gathering at Jerusalem to discuss certain doctrines. At that meeting James seems to be presiding, and he voices the final judgment (Acts 15:13-19). Some Christians have looked at this passage and jumped to the conclusion that James, therefore, must have been the pastor over the church at Jerusalem. In reality, James was an apostle, for Paul wrote in Galatians 1:19, "But I did not see any other of the apostles except James the Lord's brother." We see here that an *apostle* headed up the church at Jerusalem, not a pastor. However, if we cannot see beyond our present-day church structure, we will not be able to recognize this truth.

Another example of how our modern conception of the church limits our understanding of the New Testament wineskin is the way we look at Timothy. Many Bible teachers today refer to 1 and 2 Timothy (along with Titus) as the *pastoral epistles*, and they interpret the writings as if Paul was writing to the pastor Timothy. Consequently, all the instructions given by Paul to Timothy are thought to be directives to pastors. Such an understanding is false and reveals how easily our interpretations of Scripture can be influenced by our own experiences in our traditional church structure of today. The truth is that Timothy was an apostle, not a pastor. We know this because the first letter to the Thessalonians begins with, "Paul and Silvanus and Timothy to the church..." (1 Thess. 1:1). Throughout this letter, the words *we* and *us* are used to refer to these three men, who were working together. Then in 2:6 we read: "...nor did we seek glory from men, either from you or from others, even though as apostles of Christ we might have asserted our authority." If the Word of God tells us that Timothy was anointed as an apostle, then we should not think of him as a pastor. Confirmation of this calling can be found in 1 Timothy 1:18, where we see that Timothy was "sent out" through prophecy, just as Paul was earlier (Acts 13:2-3). Seeing this, we must recognize that 1 and 2 Timothy are instructions for apostles, not for pastors. This will change much of our understanding of church structure.

It is important to see this distinction in the roles of the apostles and pastors because we must not let our evaluations of the New Testament church be clouded by expectations based on present-day organizational structures. If we had never in our lives experienced a modern-day church, and all we had in our hands was a Bible to decide how things should function, we immediately would recognize the roles of apostles and prophets at the forefront — not pastors

— and we would see God's design in a totally new light. We must take that fresh, new perspective as we look in the Bible.

CHAPTER 8

HEADSHIP
IN THE LOCAL CHURCH

The most prominent people in the New Testament Church were apostles. They were the "sent ones." Paul spoke of this apostolic authority when he wrote, "...as apostles of Christ we might have asserted our authority" (1 Thess. 2:6). Notice that they had authority because they had been sent directly by Christ. First Corinthians 12:28 tells us, "And God has appointed in the church, first apostles...." The New Testament makes God's order for the Church clear.

The authority of the apostle was in line with the work God had called him to do. For example, Paul held authority over the churches he had founded among the Gentiles, yet he went before the apostles at Jerusalem with a submissive attitude (Gal. 2:2). We can also learn from Paul's explanation to the Corinthian believers how his authority reached to them because he had labored among them as an apostle, however he also said that his authority did *not* reach beyond those places where he had already worked (II Cor. 10:13-16). An apostle did not have an all-inclusive dominion, but only the authority that corresponded to his direct commission from God.

The apostles were in fellowship with and submission to one another. The apostle Paul rebuked the apostle Peter, correcting his hypocrisy (Gal. 2:2,9). They were not totally independent, but they relied upon each other.

As we study the New Testament, we see that after the apostles established a work, they appointed *elders* to oversee the church. In Acts 14:23 we read that Paul and Barnabas "appointed elders for them in every church, having prayed with fasting." Notice that this was their practice in *every* city.

It is important that we recognize that elders were chosen by an apostle. In 1 Timothy 3:1-7, we can read how the apostle Paul instructed the apostle Timothy to choose elders to oversee the church at Ephesus. Similarly, Paul instructed the apostle Titus to "appoint elders in every city..." throughout the island of Crete (Titus 1:5). Elders were not elected, voted in, nor appointed by an organization. They were chosen and appointed by an apostle.

Do not let the terminology confuse you. The word *elder* was used in Bible times in two different ways. First, the term simply meant *a mature or elderly man.* In the context of church government the term *elder* came to refer to those mature men who had been selected and appointed for leadership and to help oversee a church.

(Now in pointing out that older men were given the primary leadership positions, I am not trying to say anything negative about women nor young people in church leadership today. We simply are examining the New Testament Church, and if we are going to be honest with the historical and cultural setting of the Jewish people of that time period, we must note that the mature men were given most — but not all — leadership positions. In later parts of this book we will consider the wineskin of our day and how this relates to young people and women. Here we simply are attempting to study the authority structure which existed in the New Testament Church.)

From the mature men in a congregation, elders were chosen by an apostle to oversee the church. Paul gave Timothy clear guidelines on how to select the overseers. He wrote:

> An overseer, then, must be above re-proach, the husband of one wife, temper-ate, prudent, respectable, hospitable, able to teach, not addicted to wine or pugnacious, but gentle, uncontentious, free from the love of money. He must be one who manages his own household well, keeping his children under control with all dignity (but if a man does not know how to manage his own household, how will he take care of the church of God?); and not a new convert, lest he become conceited and fall into the con-demnation incurred by the devil. And he must have a good reputation with those outside the church, so that he may not fall into reproach and the snare of the devil (I Tim. 3:2-7).

Titus was given similar instruction by Paul on how to select elders to oversee the churches (Titus 1:5-9). Only men with proven Christian character were to be selected to serve as overseers.

Note that the chosen and appointed elders were also called *overseers*. As a group they were referred to as the *presbytery*.

The primary responsibilities of the elders of a church included protecting the flock from false doctrine and teaching the congregation what is true (Acts 20:28-30; 1 Tim. 5:17). Peter wrote:

> Therefore, I exhort the elders...shepherd the flock of God among you, not under compulsion, but voluntarily, according to the will of God; and not for sordid gain, but with eagerness; nor yet as lording it over those allotted to your charge, but proving to be examples to the flock (1 Pet. 5:1-3).

Elders gave direction, care, and leadership as shepherds would to their own flocks, making sure they were fed, kept in good health, and protected from danger.

To summarize, we could say that in New Testament times an apostle was sent by God to establish and lay a foundation for a specific work. Once the work was stable, the apostle chose a group of elders to oversee the congregation.

The work of the apostle was not finished just because the presbytery had been established. In the New Testament we see two different courses of action being taken. The apostle Paul left the churches he had founded in the hands of elders, but he maintained relationships with those churches, returning for visits, writing letters, sending his attendants, and giving directions. Exactly how much authority over the churches he kept, we do not know for sure, but in his letters we can see that he definitely expected some form of ongoing respect (1 Thess. 2:6; 2 Cor. 13:10).

Other apostles never left the work they had founded. For example, James was the apostle who continued overseeing the work at Jerusalem. Peter continued ruling over the church at Antioch for many years. The apostle Timothy appointed elders over the church at Ephesus, but he remained there for years, overseeing the work of the elders, who were directly under his authority.

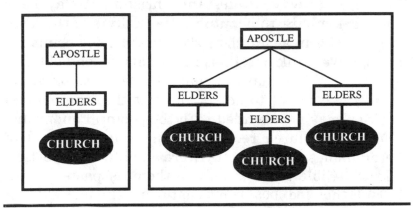

TWO KINDS OF ROLES FOR APOSTLES

When an apostle remained as head over a local church, he sometimes was considered a part of the presbytery, and at other times he kept his distinct identity. In Acts 15, five references are made to "the apostles and the elders." There the apostles are considered a separate group. In other Scripture passages the apostles are included with the elders. Peter even identifies himself as a fellow elder (1 Pet. 5:1). Of course, every apostle should meet the qualifications required for eldership. Either way we look at it, it is scripturally accurate to include or exclude the leading apostle from the presbytery.

It is vital to note here that the apostles who were called to minister at one location did not become pastors. Christians today have been trained to think that every senior minister over a local church should be called a pastor. This is foolish. It reminds me of something in my own history: I was raised as a Roman Catholic, and for months after I became a Protestant, I still thought of the ministers as priests; I had a difficult time not calling the minister "Father." In the same way, Protestant Christians today have one-track minds: they automatically think of the leading minister in a church as a pastor. This is primarily because we think in terms of positions instead of God's anointings. It is hard for most Protestants to reprogram their minds to accept the fact that the leading position may not be filled with the pastoral anointing. The Early Church recognized anointings. Men like Peter, James, and Timothy were anointed as apostles, and the Bible never refers to them as pastors even though they led local congregations. The fact that an apostle remained in one location did not mean he had lost his anointing or had become a pastor. Apostles remained apostles. Pastors were pastors. They are two different callings and anointings.

We need to break free of our traditional concepts of how the church should be organized. Let's take a fresh, unhindered look at the Bible.

An apostle, with a group of elders (known as the presbytery), was in charge of each local congregation. The apostle James was the senior minister at Jerusalem. The apostle Peter was the head of the church at Antioch. Timothy was the apostle of the church at Ephesus. At least for a time, Apollos was the apostle who followed Paul at Corinth. Too often we have rejected the apostolic position, or pushed the apostles out of the local church setting, thinking they were traveling ministers only. Indeed, some apostles travel, as Paul did, in keeping with their callings. However, the typical structure of the local church in the New Testament consisted of a group of elders sharing in the oversight of the congregation, but under the headship of an apostle.

Before we take a closer look at the presbytery, let's consider one other position in the church: that of *deacon*. The word deacon means "servant." The qualifications for deacons are listed in 1 Timothy 3:8-13. We see in Acts 6:1-6 that deacons were selected by the congregation with the approval of the apostles. The deacon position is an honored one, but one of servanthood, not authority. Deacons are not part of the presbytery, but they are dedicated Christians who serve the elders and the entire congregation.

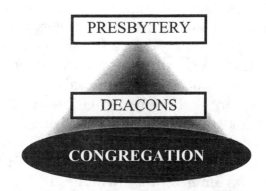

THE NEW TESTAMENT STRUCTURE

We must identify both the deacon and elder roles as *positions* in the local church. *Positions* are different than *anointings.* Anointings are supernatural endowments from God. There are many anointings. In contrast, there are only two positions that we see established in the New Testament church: the position of *elder* and the position of *deacon.*

Another important difference between positions and anointings is that believers place other believers in church positions, while only God gives anointings: apostles appoint elders and the congregation chooses deacons, but only God can impart gifts to believers. Another difference is that believers have the authority to remove other believers from positions, but no one can take away another believer's anointing. If an apostle removes someone from the position of elder, that elder no longer has authority as an elder. However, if that elder has a gift from God, no one can take that gift away. Positions are offices within the church, while gifts are God-given anointings.

What we need to see clearly is that the various anointings were represented among the leadership in the New Testament Church. We can compare this biblical structure with a present-day corporation: several businesspeople may serve in positions of authority, but each of them may have an area of expertise such as finances, public relations, sales, and so on. In a similar fashion, God has designed the church so that a group of elders oversees it, but each elder has God-given gifts.

If we take a closer look at the Church in the New Testament, we immediately will be able to identify various anointings among the elders. For example, in Acts 13:1 we read, "Now there were at Antioch, in the church that was there, prophets and teachers: Barnabas and Simeon who was called Niger, and Lucius of Cyrene, and Manaen...and Saul." Notice that believers anointed as prophets and teachers were among the eldership of the local church. The Jerusalem church had more than one apostle, plus Judas and Silas, who were prophets, along with many other elders (Acts 15:4, 22, 23). Some of the elders may have had one of the five ministry gifts, and others may have had other anointings, as we will see in the next chapter.

CHAPTER 9

AUTHORITY AMONG
THE PRESBYTERY

Now for a vital truth that will clear up much confusion in church structure: God correlates an elder's anointing to authority. I will repeat that statement because it is one of the most important principles in this book: *God correlates an elder's anointing to authority.* There is a God-ordained order among the elders of the church. Let's analyze this order according to the New Testament.

Some Christians may try to look for an authority structure in Ephesians 4:11, where the ministry gifts (apostle, prophet, evangelist, pastor, and teacher) are listed. But to look at this Scripture in this way is wrong because no authority structure is implied: we are not told in the verse that the apostle has more authority than the prophet, and the prophet more than the evangelist. It would be presumptuous to say that the listing indicates a hierarchy of roles. Furthermore, the New Testament contains contradictions to this list that imply a different order of authority; for example, Philip was an evangelist, but he appears to have no authority in his local church other than as a deacon. Evidently God did not intend for us to look at Ephesians 4:11 for His structure of authority.

A different verse, however, clearly states God's order for church leadership. First Corinthians 12:28

tells us: "And God has appointed in the church, first apostles, second prophets, third teachers, then miracles, then gifts of healings, helps, administrations, various kinds of tongues." No other passage in the Bible gives an order to the gifts. Therefore, we must look carefully here to see what God is trying to tell us.

Some Christians may react negatively to the concept of any "hierarchy" existing in the Early Church. There has been much abuse of authority in some present-day churches, and I do not wish to excuse it or open the door for future misuses. I want to avoid implying any domineering image of church leadership. Also, I am being careful with the words I use in communicating to you about this subject. Terms like submission have different meanings to different Christians. To call one gift "higher" or "greater" than another may cause some readers to reject the entire contents of this book. Even though these words are in the Bible, when they are used in the wrong context they become bondage-creating tools of the devil. If I could convince you that I am implying authority only as the Holy Spirit directs it, I am sure you would consider freely what I am about to say. Since I cannot communicate completely beyond the personal experiences you have had in your own church, good or bad, I will trust the Spirit of God, Whom we share, to override my limited ability.

In the context of I Corinthians 12:28, Paul is saying that the Body of Christ has many parts. He is explaining how all the various members of the Body fit together without division so that they can operate in unity, each benefiting and honoring the others. It is the Holy Spirit who places us in the Church where He wishes, and by His sovereignty He has placed apostles first, prophets second, and so on. Make no mistake about this fact: God has appointed a particular design for His Church.

In 1 Corinthians 12:28 the gifts that are listed first are referred to in the Greek in verse 31 as *meizon*, which is translated as "greater" or "higher." Although we do not want to elevate the people with these anointings in an unscriptural way, we should not be afraid to use the very terms God uses in the Bible. It is unfortunate that some people would take the word *higher* to mean "worthy of praise" or "more important." In the context, Paul taught the exact opposite, saying that the higher gifts should never be exalted above the lesser gifts. In fact, we should "bestow more abundant honor" on "those members of the Body, which we deem less honorable" (1 Cor. 12:23). In other passages Paul says that those with anointings such as that of apostle will be humbled, exhibited in this world as "last of all," "fools for Christ's sake," and "without honor" (1 Cor. 4:9-10). Therefore, we must understand that God's order listed in 1 Corinthians 12:28 is not for Christians to exalt themselves, but for our recognition of God's design. Some gifts are higher or greater, but only in the Holy Spirit's authority structure — never in the sense of receiving human praise.

We will discuss humility and the proper attitudes of leaders in more detail later, but we first must understand these anointings in the proper sense. There is an order in the Body of Christ:

Apostles — Prophets — Teachers —
Workers of Miracles — Gifts of Healing
— Helps — Administrations — Tongues

In the true biblical sense, the gifts listed first are higher or greater than the gifts listed last. Christians even are exhorted twice in the context to desire earnestly these "higher" or "greater" gifts. The person who speaks in tongues should desire the gift of administrations. The one with the gift of healing should pray earnestly for miracles. A prophet must desire the apostolic anointing. This is God's order.

This order of authority is exactly what we see in the New Testament. As we discuss briefly each of these "authority" gifts, we will consider some examples from the New Testament, and see that these gifts formed the wineskin of the Early Church.

The first in the order of authority are apostles. In the Early Church, the apostles appointed elders as overseers, made decisions for the whole Church, and oversaw individual congregations.

Prophets are second. Today, most churches that accept prophets place them in submission to the pastor. This is unscriptural, and it grieves the Holy Spirit. When the prophets in the Old Testament speak to the shepherds, they demand submission from them (for example, see Ezek. 34:1-10). In Acts 13:1-3 the prophets and teachers at the Antioch church send out Paul and Barnabas without any pastor involved. This does not mean that every prophet has authority over every pastor; however, a prophet who is a part of the presbytery, and who is accepted as a prophet to the church, does have authority over a pastor. (It is worth reiterating here that some senior ministers currently being called "pastor" really are anointed as apostles; in that case a prophet should submit to their "pastor.") First Corinthians 14:32 tells us that "the spirits of prophets are subject to prophets." Therefore, prophets must submit to each other. Also, since they are second in authority, they should submit to directives from apostles.

Teachers are third. This category does not include every Sunday school or Bible study teacher. We are referring to an office recognized by the church whereby an anointed teacher is placed among the presbytery. Notice that it is the teachers who are with the prophets when they send Paul and Barnabas to the mission field (Acts 13:1-3). Teachers must be submitted to apostles and prophets, and yet be willing to work alongside other teachers.

Miracle workers are important as the fourth level of authority. Miracles often are used in the New Testament as confirmation of God's authority. Paul and Barnabas justify their position by "relating what signs and wonders God had done through them among the Gentiles" (Acts 15:12). Who is going to argue with a person through whom God does miracles? An elder with a gift of miracles is to be recognized above those with lesser anointings.

The fifth gift is that of healing. In the same way that miracles are confirmations of God's authority, so also is healing power.

The sixth gift is that of helps. Although the Bible does not describe this gift, I will explain how I understand it. I do not see helps as the servant position in which Christians clean the church, run the nursery, or do carpentry. It would make no sense to place that type of gift above administrations. I see this gift as the anointed position in which a person stands alongside and serves, in a very personal way, an apostle or prophet. Most true apostles or prophets need a helper, much like Elijah had Elisha as his servant.

That helper needs to have authority in the church, and especially over the administrations, because the helper knows personally how to serve the needs of the apostle or prophet. An example from the New Testament is Tychicus, whom Paul describes as "our beloved brother and faithful servant" (Col. 4:7). Paul sends Tychicus to the church at Ephesus (Eph. 6:21), to the church at Colosse (Col. 4:7), and to the church at Crete (Titus 3:12) in order to carry his letters and to give further instructions. Tychicus ministers under Paul's authority, and hence he carries authority over many of the other elders he visits. This is the ministry of helps.

Administrations is next. This title is also interpreted as "leader" or "one who governs." It refers to a person who is not only gifted at organization, but who is anointed for delegating responsibilities and directing groups of people. Paul writes to Timothy about those "elders who rule well" (1 Tim. 5:17) and says they should be considered worthy of double honor. It was the administrators who ruled over the practical ministries of the local church. They had authority under the apostles, prophets, teachers, and those with gifts of miracles, healings, and helps.

The final gift is that of tongues. This is the least of the gifts in authority.

These eight gifts delineate God's order among leaders, or elders, in the local church. It is helpful to note that in 1 Corinthians 12:28 Paul assigns a definite order to the first three gifts — apostle, prophet, and teacher — and he even gives them numbers. But he does not give numbers to the gifts of miracles, healing, helps, administrations, and tongues. Instead, he simply lists them by saying, "*then* miracles, *then* gifts of healing" (italics added), and so on. Paul's use of the indefinite ordering for these last five gifts implies that we should not assume a strict descending order. We do recognize the apostle, prophet, and teacher as first, second, and third, respectively, but the remaining five gifts are not necessarily positioned so definitely.

We also should note that the first three gifts — apostle, prophet, and teacher — stand out in a distinct manner. In other Bible passages we see these three gifts specifically being named among the church leadership. Christians with gifts of miracles, healings, helps, administrations, and tongues may or may not be part of the presbytery. The three highest gifts definitely are among the presbytery.

In 1 Corinthians 12:11-28, we are told that the Holy Spirit places us in the Body where He chooses, and that He has chosen to place apostles first, prophets second, teachers third, and so on. This is the pattern of authority evident in the Early Church.

One point needs to be reemphasized here. The order of authority is determined by anointings "among the elders in the presbytery." A Christian who has received a gift may never have held an eldership position because of a lack of spiritual maturity. Paul gave Timothy clear guidelines for choosing elders on the basis of Christian maturity, stability, and proven character (I Tim. 3:1-7). If a leader had fallen short in his own life, he never would have received a position of authority among the presbytery. It was not enough just to be anointed by the Spirit. Proven character, plus an anointing, established one's authority.

Imagine now a church with all eight authority gifts. Let's say this church has an apostle who was sent directly by God to accomplish a specific work. Let's say there are one or more anointed prophets who could identify attacks of the enemy, correct the congregation when it got off course, confront sin, and speak the Word of God with power. Let's say there are several teachers who are able to impart truth and break bondages off the people; that there are leaders with the gifts of miracles and healings, helps ministers serving and relaying directives from the apostles and prophets, and administrators overseeing every practical aspect of the ministry; and that there are several other leaders, filled with the Spirit of God, who are bathing the church in prayer. Picture such a group of leaders seeking and serving God together. Can you imagine how that church would be? The gates of hell could not prevail against the anointings working together! Those are the kinds of elders you would like to call on if you were sick (James 5:14-15). No wonder the Early Church "turned the world upside down" (Acts 17:6, KJV) in a few short years. That is the concept of team ministry that God first established in His Church.

CHAPTER 10

THE ROLE OF
THE EVANGELISTS

Where do the evangelists fit in? They are not mentioned in 1 Corinthians 12:28, which gives order to the church. Why?

The book of Acts mentions one Christian who was called an evangelist. That was Philip. Timothy was told by Paul to "do the work of an evangelist" (2 Tim. 4:5), but that was not his primary anointing; remember that we all are called to evangelize, but only a few of us are anointed as evangelists. And so, as we look at our only New Testament example, we see Philip. What does he do? We first see him as a deacon in his own church, and then we read about him preaching in Samaria with tremendous miracles and many people getting saved (Acts 8:4-12). Philip does not stay long in Samaria, but the apostles Peter and John immediately come down from Jerusalem to carry on with and establish the work (Acts 8:14-25). In the meantime, the Holy Spirit removes Philip from Samaria and puts him on the road to preach to an Ethiopian eunuch (Acts 8:26-28). Then the Spirit of God suddenly snatches Philip away: "But Philip found himself at Azotus; and as he passed through he kept preaching the gospel to all the cities, until he came to Caesarea"

(Acts 8:40). Notice that Philip does not stay long in those cities. God does not use him to stay and establish churches or even to do extensive follow-up. Although Philip is involved in his local church, he does not get his every move approved by the leaders of that church. The Spirit moves him about freely and quickly to wherever he is needed to preach the gospel. That is what we see as the ministry of the New Testament evangelist.

God wants evangelists to be free. He left evangelists off the list of authority gifts because He does not want evangelists to be restricted to a rulership position. God's intention for evangelists is evangelism — not the supervision of a local church.

From experience, I know that most, if not all, true evangelists are active, aggressive individuals: they like to see mass salvations and quick results. That is how God made them. Evangelists find it difficult to remain in one location, building on the same work, year after year. Usually when we try to make evangelists slow down, we grieve the Holy Spirit. Evangelists should function as Philip did, traveling freely and going where the Spirit directs. Evangelists are called to the world. Of course, they may serve as deacons and should be considered part of the congregation, but their anointings are for the salvation of souls. Evangelists must be among the lost.

Nowhere in the Bible are we told how many anointed soul-winners should be among a group of believers. We are told only to pray that the Lord would send more laborers to the harvest. How blessed would be the church that had five, ten, twenty, or more evangelists!

CHAPTER 11

THE ROLE OF
THE PASTORS

Before we identify the role of the pastor within the church, we need to look a little closer at the pastoral anointing. Remember that we are not talking about the leader today who normally heads up a church, preaches, and organizes. We are looking through God's eyes, at God's anointings. The ministry gift of pastor is the anointing that causes people to be supernaturally drawn out of the world and into the Body of Christ. Three characteristics need to be described concerning this gift.

First, the pastoral anointing establishes a certain kind of relationship between pastors and those they lead. God causes people to hear the voice of the shepherd. There is a supernatural trust placed in the sheep for their human shepherds. The sheep go to their shepherds for counseling and direction and receive a sense of security and warmth. The shepherds are the ones the sheep go to when they are in need. Leaders who are true pastors, and not "hirelings," are committed to those God has given them. This is a God-ordained relationship.

Second, we must realize that pastors are limited in the number of people for whom they can care. The pastor-sheep relationship requires time, personal contact, involvement with family members, availability for counseling, and more. No human being can have that kind of relationship with very many people. There are just not enough hours in a day. I have seen that the active pastor can shepherd about fifty people; I dare say that it is impossible to pastor (in the biblical sense of the word) many more people than that. It takes the average pastor today about sixty hours per week just to keep fifty people in a congregation. Every seasoned pastor has seen that when ten new people join the church, ten others will somehow drift away in a short time. Large numbers may go through the average church, but the pastor-led church remains approximately the same size year after year.

You may object to what I am saying here because you are thinking about churches that are larger than fifty people. If you identify the anointings of the head ministers of those large congregations, however, you will discover that even though they may be called "pastor," they actually are anointed as apostles, prophets, teachers, or administrators. Leaders with those kinds of anointings have different kinds of relationships with the people; those relationships are not as intimate, and they can include larger numbers. For example, an anointed administrator can organize and direct hundreds or even thousands of people. A teacher may instruct a huge group on a regular basis. Prophets and apostles also can exhort or minister to large crowds. In contrast, pastors are not just in the business of organizing, directing, teaching, or exhorting; pastors must pastor, and that requires time with each individual. As a consequence, the pastoral anointing is limited in the number of people to whom each pastor can minister.

Next, let me point out the pastoral need for a spiritual head. As I have traveled and ministered to churches all over the world, I have observed that every pastor who is really anointed as a pastor draws spiritual strength from an apostle or prophet. Whether or not pastors will admit it, they read the books, listen to the teaching tapes or radio programs, and receive whatever strength they can from strong leaders. Many pastors today rely on Oral Roberts, some on Kenneth Hagin, others on David Wilkerson, Jack Hayford, John Wimber, or Dr. David Yonggi Cho. Some pastors draw strength from men and women of God from generations past, and others depend on the leaders within their denominations. Without regular times of getting away from their local ministries and going to conferences or conventions, pastors cannot survive spiritually. In contrast, apostles and prophets may fellowship with one another, but because of their direct call from God, they do not depend on a spiritual figure ahead of them. Every pastor will die spiritually without an apostle or prophet to whom he can look.

The apostolic or prophetic influence upon pastors must not be minimized. When pastors change their focus from one apostle to another, their entire ministries change. I can remember how, when I was pastoring, I changed my "spiritual draw" from one leader to another, and my emphasis in preaching dramatically shifted, my relationships with people were altered, and even my weekly schedule changed. As a result, the congregation went through an upheaval, with many people leaving and others taking their places. All pastors are anointed by God to draw people, but what they do with those people is determined to a large extent by the apostles or prophets from whom they draw strength and direction.

The pastor's need for a spiritual head has made me look more closely at the relationship between the pastor and the apostle and between the pastor and the prophet. I have had to conclude that every pastor should be in submission to an apostle and/or a prophet. This is not an issue of forcing pastors under a spiritual head. It is, instead, the need for pastors to recognize God's design for His Body and then to flow with His plan. It is wrong for a pastor to draw spiritual strength from an apostle or prophet and not be willing to submit to that head.

What, then, is the role of the pastor in the church? There is only one passage in the New Testament that speaks about pastors, and there we are told that they are part of a team — a team of ministry gifts — that equips the saints for the work of service (Eph. 4:11-12). Pastors are in the business of "equipping." And they are to work together with those having other ministry gifts.

In addition, we can look in the Old Testament where God rebukes the shepherds of the day. The passage gives us a clear picture of what He expects them to do:

> "Should not the shepherds feed the flock?...Those who are sickly you have not strengthened, the diseased you have not healed, the broken you have not bound up, the scattered you have not brought back, nor have you sought for the lost....And they were scattered for lack of a shepherd, and they became food

for every beast of the field and were scattered. My flock wandered through all the mountains and on every high hill, and My flock was scattered over all the surface of the earth; and there was no one to search or seek for them....And My shepherds did not search for My flock...and did not feed My flock..." (Ezekiel 34:2-8).

Of course, we cannot assume that these Old Testament shepherds are the exact counterpart of the New Testament pastors. However, this passage illustrates God's primary concern. Our Lord expects His leaders to feed the sheep and to strengthen the weak and sick; but above all else He expects them to seek out, find, and gather in those sheep that have scattered or have strayed away.

Notice that these expectations exactly correspond to the anointing of a pastor as we explained earlier. The calling of pastors, in addition to being equippers alongside other anointed ministers, is to use their anointings for gathering in the sheep.

Where can we find that role in the New Testament Church? When we study the early believers, we notice that they had two primary meeting centers. Following the report of Pentecost day, we read, "And day by day continuing with one mind in the temple, and breaking bread from house to house, they were taking their meals together with gladness and sincerity of heart, praising God..." (Acts 2:46-47). When they came together in the temple, the apostles were ministering and leading, along with the prophets and teachers. The other believers also met regularly in smaller

71

groups in homes. History indicates that, shortly after the birth of Christianity, the church at Jerusalem had approximately 100,000 people, the church at Antioch had about 30,000, and the Corinthian believers numbered approximately 60,000. It would have been impossible for the apostles to be personally involved in all the ministry necessary for those people. Who do you think presided over the meetings "from house to house"? Nowhere in the New Testament is the title of pastor given to those leaders of the smaller groups. However, they were recognized. For example, Paul wrote greetings to Priscilla and Aquila and also to "the church that is in their house" (Rom. 16:5). While the larger ministry of the apostles, prophets, and teachers was being carried out, ministry also was going on in smaller groups.

Since we can find no example in the New Testament of a pastor leading a local church or participating among the presbytery of a church, where does the pastor fit in? And why did God not list the gift of pastor among the authority gifts in 1 Corinthians 12:28? God's intention was that pastors work among the sheep, not rule over the local church. As the evangelist is to be among the unsaved, the pastor must be among the congregation. The pastor's primary role is that of gathering in the sheep.

In Acts we get the impression that the believers were meeting in many homes. Each city had a team of elders — including an apostle, prophets, teachers, and so on — and under that leadership were numerous smaller groups carrying on more personal, intimate ministries. These groups were led by those anointed as pastors. There was not just one pastor for a church, but many working among the congregation.

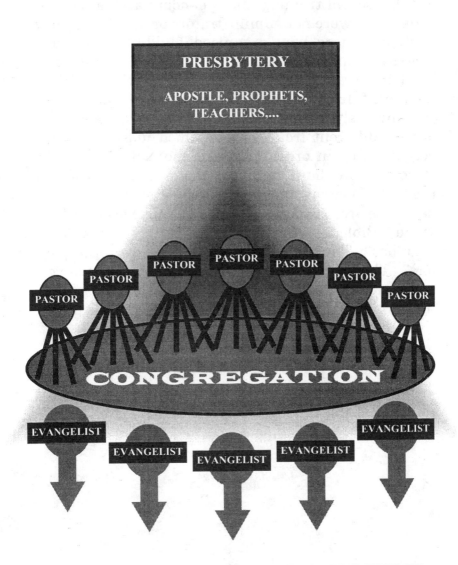

Notice that pastors were not those with four years of Bible school training and a denominational certificate. They were not administrators or apostles. They were not those who organized building programs, oversaw finances, preached on Sunday mornings, and lived in parsonages. They were Christians with a unique gift from God and hearts to love people.

Obviously, this New Testament church structure is very different from that to which most of us are accustomed. In order to accept the New Testament structure, we have to move the pastor out of the position of senior minister. We must stop calling the head minister "pastor." Let's open our eyes and look in our Bibles. Who were the heads of the local churches? The apostles were. Where were the pastors? They were not in rulership positions. Are you willing to break free of the mind-set developed among traditional churchgoers today and begin to accept the New Testament structure?

This is it.

Part Three

Two Thousand Years
of
Wineskin Stretching

CHAPTER 12

ADVANCING
TOWARD MATURITY

We have taken a look at the Church in the New Testament. Now let's look at the Church over the course of history. During the last two thousand years the Church has gone through countless changes. There have been mighty moves of God's Spirit in various places around the world. Leaders anointed as apostles and prophets frequently have arisen to alter the course of Christianity. Almost every Christian denomination began in an explosion of activity and controversy. There also have been periods of silence and apathy. Various groups have emerged with great zeal, only to be unnoticed a few years later. Understanding these historical shifts — and the roles that the apostles and prophets have played in them — will challenge us and demand that we reevaluate the direction of our lives.

God has a plan. He is preparing a people with whom He can spend eternity. He is raising a Bride for His Son. Ephesians 4:11-13 speaks about the saints maturing, attaining unity, and growing into the fullness of Christ. Paul also explains to the Christians at Ephesus:

77

> "...You are fellow-citizens with the saints, and are of God's household, having been built upon the foundation of the apostles and prophets, Christ Jesus Himself being the corner stone, in whom the whole building, being fitted together is growing into a holy temple in the Lord...into a dwelling of God in the Spirit." (Eph. 2:19-22).

The Church is "growing into a holy temple." We are being carried along according to God's preordained plan, with the goal that we are going to rise into the fullness of Christ (see also, Eph. 3:9-10).

This does not mean that the Church will take over the world. On the contrary, the world will grow more evil and wicked as we draw nearer to the end. It is when darkness covers the earth that the glory of God will shine brightest upon the Church (Is. 60:2). The Church will get holier and holier while the world becomes darker and darker.

The progress of the Church toward maturity can be seen as we study Church history.

Throughout the last two thousand years God raised up great men and women to proclaim biblical truths to the masses. In the last five hundred years Martin Luther, John Calvin, John Wesley, and others each brought messages of life to the Church. People's eyes were opened supernaturally to see the hope of salvation through faith and other biblical truths, such as holiness and the priesthood of the believers. In the twentieth century God has opened our understanding to things like the baptism of the Holy Spirit, tongues, healing, worship, discipleship, Body ministry, church growth, and faith. The Bride is being perfected through God's work of revealing scriptural truths. God is also empowering us to walk in those truths. He is enabling the Church, one step at a time, to move closer to the promised position of the fullness of Christ.

The progress of the Church has not been continuous nor smooth. Each time that God has revealed a truth, it has taken time for people to accept it. Usually the first messengers of those truths received great persecution and rejection. Finally, the people began to accept the teachers as the Holy Spirit enabled them. This has happened repeatedly with each step upward. We often call these steps "moves of God" or "waves of the Spirit." After each move of God, another one follows as God transforms us from glory to glory.

CHAPTER 13

THE BIRTH OF A CHRISTIAN ORGANIZATION

Preceding every move of God, there is a *hunger* that grows in the hearts of men and women. They become dissatisfied with the spiritual conditions around them. They begin to cry out to God in prayer. A God-ward earnestness develops in them, and the cares of the world fade into insignificance. When the number of hungry souls increases, "the fullness of times comes," and then God pours out His Spirit on the thirsty hearts.

When new wine is poured out, *new leaders* suddenly appear. We must not overlook this step in each of God's outpourings. Many Christians would prefer to look for some mystical force that creates revival. Or they may think that God sovereignly acts without human involvement. It is true that God works mysteriously, supernaturally, and sovereignly, but He works primarily through people. Jesus described the life of the Holy Spirit as that which flows out of *our* innermost beings (John 7:38). Peter explained the outpouring of the Spirit by quoting from the prophet Joel, through whom God said, "'...I will pour forth of my Spirit upon all mankind; and your sons and your daughters shall prophesy...'" (Acts 2:17). When God moves, ordinary people, your sons and your daughters, boldly proclaim what God instills in their spirits. When God answers the thirst of people's hearts, He does it by giving gifts to them — imparting to them scriptural revelation that provides the needed answers, and empowering them to meet the needs that are in their hearts. It is through human vessels that God works.

The first leaders to arise are anointed as prophets: "Surely the Lord God does nothing unless He reveals His secret counsel to His servants the prophets" (Amos 3:7). God begins a move by causing certain men and/or women to boldly proclaim His answers for the needs of the hour. These people speak revelation — not something beyond Scripture, but new insight into scriptural truths. They prophetically proclaim what the Spirit within them is compelling them to announce.

These proclamations often cause the wineskin to rip. The messages or revelations demand change, and sometimes existing organizations are disrupted. After awhile, those who are hungry for more of God migrate from the old wineskin into the fresh rain of the Spirit.

Then the apostles appear on the scene to establish a new wineskin. Frequently it is a prophet who receives an apostolic anointing. At other times, God chooses to send another leader independently to found the work. Leaders with gifts of teaching, administrations, and pastoring are quickly raised up. Some moves of God also have included evangelists and those with gifts of miracles and healing. There is much resistance and warfare in the beginning, but finally a complete wineskin, led by apostles, is established that is able to handle the new wine from above.

Nearly every major denomination and Christian organization has appeared through a genesis like this. Whether we are speaking of the original Church in Acts, the Lutheran denomination, the Salvation Army, the Foursquare Church, the Jesus Movement, or organizations such as The Full Gospel Business Men's Fellowship, they all have gone through a similar progression from a hunger in people's hearts, to an outpouring of the Holy Spirit, to new prophetic leaders, to an apostle, to a new wineskin. This is the pattern we see of God's outpourings throughout the Church's history and continuing in our day.

CHAPTER 14

THE AGING OF
A WINESKIN

When a new wineskin is forming under an outpouring of God's Spirit, the Church enjoys great blessings. Souls are saved. Individuals grow strong in faith. Answers to prayers seem more immediate and powerful. Zealous leaders go out to carry forth the Gospel.

But gradually the ministry goes through a major metamorphosis. Those with apostolic or prophetic gifts retire, die or simply are replaced. As those with the original callings from God drift into the background, new leaders move into their positions . Often the key leadership position is held by a teacher for awhile, but soon *the control invariably ends up in the hands of those with gifts of administrations*, with pastors serving under them. The apostolic anointing is replaced by superintendents, district representatives, overseers, bishops and others with various titles, all of whom have administrative hearts. The prophetic voice is replaced by doctrinal statements and accepted forms of practice. Evangelists last for a time, but eventually they too are eliminated. The pastors then are exalted, and they begin working with administrators.

The Holy Spirit flows through administrators in ways that cause things to be organized and structured. The heartfelt desire of administrators is to help everything run smoothly and efficiently. Because administrators are in charge, the focus of ministries becomes whatever is practical, efficient, and financially feasible. Direction comes not so much through inspiration as through reason. Much practical thinking replaces great faith. The movement of God is transformed from a flowing spiritual Body into a mechanistic organization.

This is not to say that administrators are bad. They simply are doing what they are anointed to do. Because they are not apostles or prophets, they are incapable of hearing God's message, as apostles, or speaking out, as prophets. They have no God-empowering to do the greater works. Their minds are organization-centered and program-centered. This is the anointing of administrators, and this is how the Spirit of God works through them.

With an administrator at the head of a ministry, the greater anointings are restricted. Jesus said that no one can rise above the level of one's leaders (Luke 6:40; Matt. 10:24-25). Administrations is one of the lesser gifts, and thus it is difficult for new apostles or prophets to arise under administrators. If an apostle steps out with God-given instructions for a radical new direction, the administrator's smooth-running programs are disrupted. Those with the gifts of miracles and healing have little place in the world of administrators; the "unproductive" hours in fasting and prayer even may seem foolish to them. It makes no sense to the administrators that those gifted in helps would "waste their lives" in service to apostles or prophets. Administrators like written doctrinal statements, not unpredictable prophets whom they cannot control.

In trying to further their own goals, administrators may use evangelists or prophets or those with gifts of healing. But administrators rarely understand, submit to, or fully release those people for ministry. Neither administrators nor pastors have the wisdom or spiritual power required to release the greater anointings.

Administrators cannot say the proper words to inspire the proper thoughts of a true apostle or prophet. In fact, administrators who hold the authority tend to quench the Holy Spirit working in any individual who has a greater anointing; for administrators try to make everyone think in "practical" ways, rather than in apostolic, prophetic, teaching, or miracles ways. To the apostle, they say, "That's not our vision!" To the prophet, they say, "Don't rock the boat!" To the teacher, they say, "We don't teach that!" To the worker of miracles, they say, "Produce!" And to the helps minister they say, "Get a job!"

When administrators have authority over organizations, they will allow only other administrators, whom they understand, to work with them, and pastors whom they can control, to work under them. The Holy Spirit is restricted through well-meant rules and programs. Administrators become a "lid" on the people involved under them.

Because administrators are incapable of raising up or releasing the greater anointings, there is a shift in the training of new leaders. It is the apostle who can disciple and release other individuals for ministry. The administrator, however, must depend upon

Bible schools and established patterns of education. Such systems of training can give rise only to other administrators, teachers, and pastors; they have little to do with God's higher anointings. Apostles are concerned primarily with spiritual maturity — knowing God and His calling. Schools emphasize knowledge, managerial skills, and practical information. As time passes, Christian organizations become more and more naturally-oriented in their training programs.

Once administrators are running an organization, the wineskin has become relatively inflexible. Ephesians 2:20 tells us that apostles and prophets lay the foundation; when they are gone, the foundation does not change. The ministry may grow in size, and it may undergo superficial modifications, but the structure remains the same. Leaders may attempt to stir up the old wine through the works of an evangelist or with new programs, but the fruits of such efforts are always short-lived and limited. A "charismatic renewal movement" among the Episcopalians may spark a little spiritual life, but on Sunday mornings that people still will be inside the same wineskin that was established hundreds of years ago. No matter what new program the Methodists sponsor, they still will be Methodists. The Lutheran Church has been the Lutheran Church for over four centuries. The Salvation Army has not experienced a major outpouring of God's Spirit since William Booth, its founder and apostle, died. Once administrators are controlling an organization and the higher anointings are eliminated, the wineskin has become inflexible. And it will remain inflexible for generations to come.

CHAPTER 15

CHANGES IN PREACHING

As the wineskin of an established ministry ages and becomes inflexible, important changes are made in preaching and teaching. Certain topics are common at the beginnings of the various moves of God while the apostles and prophets are active. Other topics are common after the wineskin is established and the organization is taken over by administrators. For example, at Pentecost, Peter gave a message of the simple truth concerning Jesus and the work of the Holy Spirit; the writer of the book of Acts recorded the results, including conviction power, mass salvations, miracles, healings, joy, boldness, radical commitment, and love demonstrated by financial generosity. These topics are the very messages that have been emphasized in the midst of every great revival over the last two thousand years.

The following table contrasts "new wine" topics with "old wine" topics. In the left column are the topics that commonly are stressed at the beginning of every move of God; in the right column are the topics frequently stressed after the apostles and prophets are gone and the wine has become old.

NEW-WINE TOPICS	OLD-WINE TOPICS
A simple message of Jesus' death and resurrection.	Intellectual and/or theological issues.
A work of the Holy Spirit: conviction power, the spiritual gifts, the leading within the individual's life, boldness, anointings, manifestations of glory, etc.	Human social duties and responsibilities: family, politics, community involvement, feeding the hungry, etc.
Sudden transformation and instantaneous conversions.	Slow, consistent, maturing and growth.
Aggressive, frequent, verbal evangelism.	Evangelism through child-rearing and community witness.
Radical discipleship: sacrifice, paying the price, forsaking all.	Commitment to the church's programs and good, moral living.
Finances: faith, selling all, risking all.	Finances: supporting the church, paying bills, being responsible.
Jesus' imminent return.	Long-range planning without thought for Jesus' return.
Miscellaneous: God's power, repentance, etc.	Miscellaneous: philosophy, ethics, psychology, etc.

These distinctions in preaching topics do not imply that one side is right while the other is wrong. All of these topics contain truths that every Christian must learn and apply. However, it is important to note *the shift in preaching emphasis* that takes place as a wineskin ages.

CHAPTER 16

THE TOTAL
WINESKIN

In addition to observing how the leadership and the preaching are incorporated within a wineskin, we could look at any aspect of a Christian endeavor. For example, we can observe a relationship between church building and the outpouring of "wine" in which they were formed.

The old Roman Catholic churches are stately Gothic cathedrals, with statues, orderly pews, and ornate altar arrangements. After the wineskin-ripping that came through Vatican II, the Catholic churches reflecting those changes and a more liberal theology were built as stylish, progressive structures with sanctuaries that look much like modern auditoriums. In contrast, many Episcopal churches are stone structures with beautiful stained-glass windows. The Presbyterians traditionally have extremely well-organized facilities that reflect the Calvinistic doctrine on which they were founded. The thousands of small Baptist churches are a demonstration of the fundamental, evangelistic theology that views the true Christians as only a few faithfuls in each area. There is another "Baptist way of thinking," held by only a few leading Baptist ministers whose evangelistic theology encompasses the entire world; their buildings are huge, practical, and modern.

The old Pentecostal churches that emphasized holiness were built with very little decor, but with high platforms from which messages were aggressively delivered to the congregations. Among these buildings were the early Assembly of God churches, but many of the present-day Assemblies have redesigned their facilities into modern, multipurpose, and less threatening styles, in keeping with the theology of the day. Methodists who have accepted a more liberal theology have modern buildings, while those still holding to traditional Methodism meet in wood-framed chapels, painted white, with a bell inside the steeple. The present "Faith" churches, along with a few other newer groups, have made abandoned warehouses and rectangular metal buildings popular for services; the movable chairs and nonrestrictive settings are evidence of specific doctrinal views and a breaking away from past religious traditions.

In the same way, parachurch organizations have meeting places that match their "wine." For example, The Full Gospel Business Men's Fellowship, which emphasizes the work of the Holy Spirit in every person's life (not just in the lives of ministers) meets outside the local church, usually in restaurants. Youth With A Mission provides training centers with live-in dormitories and classrooms, rather than sanctuaries.

In making these observations, I do not want to overemphasize the relationship between theology and building structure, since so many other factors are involved (especially the time required for change and the availability of money). However, it is clear that building design is very much influenced by the beliefs of those involved.

We also could study the different forms of worship that have arisen out of each move of the Spirit. During the Dark Ages, when the Roman Catholic clergy was aloof and distant from the common people, the worship was lofty and incomprehensible to the layperson. With Martin Luther and the Reformation, new songs sprang forth declaring the fresh revelations from above. When John Wesley boldly proclaimed a message that shocked Europe, Charles Wesley arose with corresponding hymns. William Booth brought in loud cymbals and horns to match the aggressive evangelism of the original Salvation Army. The early Pentecostals sang hymns sounding forth holiness and the power available through God. More recently the Charismatics made simple choruses popular, revealing their belief in a new freedom for all Christians. Out of the Jesus Movement hundreds of Scripture songs were born, and in the "Faith" churches confessions of faith were put to music. Each time God has stretched the wineskin of the Church, the Spirit has inspired new forms of worship to express those changes.

Many other associations between wineskins and wine could be made here. We could discuss which churches have catechism classes, which ones hold Sunday school programs, which ones choose a children's church, and which ones have Christian schools for educating their children. Which musical instruments are allowed in a church reflects that church's basic doctrinal beliefs. The ways the stage, altar, and/or pulpit are arranged are determined largely by the theology of the church. The use of hymnals, chorus books, overhead projectors, bulletins, or announcement sheets all indicate a specific wineskin.

How finances are handled, and whether funds are channeled toward missions, children, the poor, or local programs, are influenced by the underlying work of the founders. Every aspect of the wineskin is formed by the wine that originally fashioned it.

CHAPTER 17

PROBLEMS WITH
AN OLD WINESKIN

Unfortunately, the Church throughout history has attempted to capture each move of God and build a structure to contain it. Each time God has sent prophets and apostles, given new revelation, and poured out His Spirit, people have designed programs, developed doctrinal statements, constructed buildings, and organized denominations in an effort to preserve the work of God. Too often they have thought of their experience with God as the ultimate end, rather than realizing that He is taking us from glory to glory (2 Cor. 3:18). As a result, we have numerous wineskins today, but each one reflects what God did in its founding. Organization is not bad, but many Christians are locked into those wineskins, dedicated to the wine of the past, and hence oblivious to the ongoing work of God in raising up a holy Bride.

Jesus explained that those led by the Spirit will be changing and moving constantly. He said, "'The wind blows where it wishes and you hear the sound of it, but do not know where it comes from and where it is going; so is everyone who is born of the Spirit'" (John 3:8). To move with the Spirit demands constant change. Our natural tendency is contrary to God's ways. We like things stable, secure, and comfortable. But God demands freedom. His work, like the wind, never can be limited, boxed in, or confined. Our efforts to crystallize and restrict the Spirit are contrary to the ongoing work of God.

To see this clearly, let's picture in our minds what would happen if God poured new wine into a denomination run by administrators and pastors. Disaster would strike! If one hundred prophets suddenly arose within an organization, giving bold new directions, major wineskin ripping would occur. The administrators would panic, trying to keep their programs functioning, the people sedated, and everything under control. If a thousand souls suddenly were added to the average pastor-run church, the pastor would be excited for a day but then have a nervous breakdown because it is impossible for one person to care intimately for all those people. A pastor does not have the *kind of anointing* needed to oversee that many people. An administrator does not have the *kind of anointing* needed to handle prophets. Today's churches, with an administrator at the head and a wineskin that has already begun to age, could not handle God's power if He chose now to pour out His Spirit in abundance.

We must remember that changing a wineskin is not just a matter of incorporating a few new ideas. The entire wineskin is involved. If God pours out His Spirit on an established organization, He may require the administrators to humble themselves, give up their positions of authority (and the corresponding salaries), and submit to "wild" prophets and apostles, who, incidentally, are not always concerned if they have to rip up established programs from beginning to end. Then worship has to change: The pianist who has served faithfully, Sunday after Sunday, may not be too happy about that. Elders and deacons who resist must be removed. The building structure needs to be altered; the pulpit may have to be repositioned; the children's department needs to be reorganized. The finances have to be redirected. The secretary even will have to change the bulletin! *The greater the outpouring, the greater the wineskin ripping.*

Please do not think I am denouncing everything going on in our present churches and Christian organizations. Far from it! In fact, I see tremendous works of God happening today. Many people are being brought to Jesus and discipled. Devout Christians who love God are laboring with all their strength and to the best of their God-given abilities. Praise God for our brothers and sisters in Christ!

However, we need to understand certain truths so that we draw the line where God draws the line. Yes, God is working through our present wineskins. But no, His great outpouring will not be contained in any one of them.

CHAPTER 18

WHAT ABOUT YOU?

Thousands of Christians are sitting in dead churches hoping God will wake everybody up. Week after week they endure boredom, knowing deep inside that there must be more to the Christian life. They quietly blame the pastor for not praying more; they may grumble about the worship; they are frustrated with the elders; or even worse, they just sit there and accept the lie that God is going to do something someday for their church. They are waiting on God to move, while God is waiting on them to move.

It is foolish to think that God will pour out His Spirit within our established denominations — even within those that are Holy Spirit-oriented. It is not enough to believe in the Holy Spirit and desire His gifts. Administrators have taken the reins. Apostolic and prophetic voices are seldom received. It concerns me when a denomination begins losing its evangelists or allows them little time to minister. If the Holy Spirit is not being permitted to work through His gifts, then He simply is not being allowed to work. The preaching in our long-established churches now consists primarily of old-wine sermons. Things have stabilized and become comfortable. The ministers have administrative mentalities. Many of our established wineskins have become old and inflexible.

If you want new wine, you must step out of your comfortable world and go to where the Spirit is moving. This will cost you. I remember one older Christian who told me about the beginning days of the Nazarene denomination and how they all had to leave their nice, respectable church to go down to the forming Nazarene congregation, which met in a storefront building. And there the glory of God used to fall. Many of us have read of the early days in the Methodist and Baptist denominations, the Salvation Army, and each of the other organizations. All of them struggled at first. Those who participated had to step out of their comfortable, traditional world and pay a price. At first there were misunderstandings, persecutions, financial struggles, and battles, but God was moving powerfully, saving souls, and working miracles.

New wine can be found only where new wineskins are in the process of forming. You can go overseas to where new missionaries and churches are being raised, or you can go to a group of believers in your own town who are working with the unsaved and are pioneering into new territory. You will see the new wine of the Spirit being poured out only where the battle is. If you want to watch God moving, go see a new wineskin!

Your friends may not go with you. Those who are happy with the status quo will not understand. The cost may seem too big, especially because the front line of God's move is associated with new Christians, problems, and struggles. But if you want new wine, the answer is to get into your car and drive to it. To see the Spirit move, you must move with the Spirit.

It is your choice.

Part Four

The Wineskin
Now Forming

CHAPTER 19

THE LAST OUTPOURING OF WINE

Prepare to become a part of a new wineskin.

What will that wineskin be like? In these final chapters we will see God's design for the Church and how it can operate in today's world.

One clarification needs to be made before we begin: The last outpouring of God's Spirit is going to be greater than any other — even greater than the outpouring that occurred on Pentecost day. God promised to pour out His Spirit on all flesh before the return of Jesus (Acts 2:17), and hence we are to expect a mighty revival (Acts 3:21). That move of God's Spirit will be accompanied by wonders in the sky above and signs on the earth beneath (Acts 2:19). The glory of the Lord will arise upon the Church (Is. 60:2), and the Church will exercise tremendous authority. Christians will grow into maturity — into the "fullness of Christ" (Eph. 4:13). They will work together as an army, each led by the Spirit of God. The Church will be purified and brought to a position of unity and love. The last outpouring of God's Spirit will manifest the glory of God and far exceed the previous blessings already seen.

This means that the wineskin for the last outpouring must be even greater, bigger, fuller, and more complete than what was seen in the Early Church. The wineskin in the New Testament held the wine of that outpouring, but it never was meant to handle the last, greater work of God.

Of course, we need all the gifts, including those of apostle and prophet, working together. And we can learn much by studying the Early Church. We need everything that we see in the New Testament. But we will need more. It is not enough for us to try to reproduce the church structure that we see in the Bible. Some Christians today are obsessed with the idea of going back to the Early Church methods in every way. But such efforts are vain and unscriptural. God promised to do a new work in our day, involving a *greater* outpouring of His Spirit.

The wineskin of the last outpouring will have all the characteristics of the New Testament wineskin, but it will be better. In this section we will look at some of the more obvious characteristics that are essential for a *complete wineskin*. However, we must not limit our thinking to what is described here or to what we see in the Early Church. As we discuss how to apply the New Testament principles to our modern world, let's be open to all that God may do — far beyond what we presently can ask or think.

CHAPTER 20

TODAY'S LIMITING CHURCH

Today's Church needs to change. We have put chains on the people of God by restricting the various anointings. When we do not allow the gifts to operate, we grieve the Giver and limit His work among us. We must realize the seriousness of this shortcoming.

In most churches today the senior minister tends to eliminate all those with anointings that are different from his. He may not do this intentionally, but a church run by an administer trains everyone to think in practical, goal-oriented ways. The prophets and evangelists, in particular, are made to feel uncomfortable, and hence pushed out. If the leader is anointed as a pastor, then everyone is taught to be caring, intimate, and personal. In a prophet-led group (which is rare), the people who get involved are usually those with similar personalities.

In denominations that rely on Bible schools and seminaries, these forces are even greater. The apostles, prophets, miracle ministers, healing ministers, helpers, and evangelists are not spiritually designed to handle four or so years of training. An evangelist or prophet truly anointed by God rarely can sit at a desk for that many hours and stay alive spiritually. The established patterns of education tend to weed out every anointing except teachers, administrators, and pastors. Denominations, and Christianity as a whole, develop congregations that favor one anointing or another.

Here is an interesting statistic: Approximately two-thirds of all churches in America have fewer than seventy people. Does that surprise you? The reason that most churches are so small is that a pastor has been positioned as the senior minister. As I explained earlier, the pastoral anointing establishes a certain kind of intimate association with a small number of people. The active pastor only can care for about fifty people.

I believe that one of the greatest needs in America today is for pastors to function not as heads of churches, but in their God-intended positions of shepherding people. Right now in the northwestern United States, where I live, only about 20 percent of the population goes to church. That includes all churches, Christian and non-Christian. At the same time, approximately 78 percent of all Americans claim to have had a born-again experience. Of course, many of them are not truly Christians, but the evangelists through television, radio, Gospel literature, and other avenues have been doing a pretty good job of saturating our country. Yet only a small percentage of the people claiming to be born-again Christians in America go to church.

What is the anointing from God that is supposed to supernaturally solve this problem? The anointing of pastor! And where are our pastors? Well, they're heading up building programs, recruiting ushers and Sunday school teachers, cleaning the church, preparing sermons, and doing administrative work. As a former pastor who is acquainted with many other pastors, I know that very, very little of their time is available to operate in their true anointing — that of gathering in the lost sheep. Thousands of anointed pastors across the country have been bound in the traditional concept of what a pastor is, thinking that they single-handedly are to do all that the apostle, prophet, teacher, administrator, and other anointed ministers should share. There is tremendous pressure upon pastors today to dedicate their ministries to administration and the handling of finances. Consequently, we have grieved the Holy Spirit, who desires to draw the wandering masses from out of the world — the greatest burden on God's heart for His people. The harvest right now is greater than it ever has been, not just for evangelists, but for true pastors.

So long as we are able to conceive of a church only as a congregation with a pastor at the head, we will be unable to see any other design. For example, if we think there is only one pastor in a local church, we will be unable to recognize anyone else in the congregation who has the same God-given heart to care for people. In the average church of fifty people, there could be several Christians with God's gift of pastor, and each of them could be using their supernatural empowering to gather in the sheep. But our traditional concept of the church puts chains on them. The very idea that God's anointings are available to many believers is revolutionary. It can be compared with the radical changes that resulted in the Church over the last few years when we realized that any Christian can be baptized in the Holy Spirit. When this truth first became accepted in our Pentecostal churches, it went through the Church like a fire setting people aflame.

And now we must awake to the fact that not only is the gift of tongues available to any Christian, but that the other gifts — of pastor, evangelist, teacher, prophet, and apostle — are available also. Not every Christian will have one of these gifts, but I believe that right now there are thousands of believers sitting in the congregations with God's calling on their lives to pastor or to function in the other gifts. However, because of our unbiblical concept of the church, they tend to think that the only way to answer God's call is to go to Bible school, submit to a denomination, stand behind the pulpit on Sunday mornings, and live in a parsonage. Our man-made, tradition-created image leaves them sitting in the pews.

So long as the pastor is at the head of a church, ten, twenty, or thirty other pastors cannot arise in the midst of the congregation. That head pastor too easily is threatened by the idea that others may gather small flocks around them. The head pastor usually sees it as disloyalty and as a potential church split. And, indeed, it may be just that, for one pastor does not have the anointing from God to oversee other pastors. Only an administrator or an apostle can oversee pastors. As a result, we are left with a pastor running each local church and many others unable to use their gifts.

So long as we have administrators in the offices at denominational headquarters, we always will have pastors holding the local reigns. A prophet always will be faced with a tremendous, immovable mountain. An apostle will have no place to declare, "I have been sent to start something completely new!" The evangelist will be restricted, required to attend four years of Bible school, and never be allowed to follow the Spirit as freely as Philip did. The average Christian will be taught just to sit in the church and fit in with the administrator's overall goals.

Of course, these flaws are unintentional. But they are inescapable with the administrator- and pastor-run organizations. Administrators are not consciously trying to eliminate the other gifts. They simply are trying to help everything flow smoothly, and they usually have good hearts in doing their work. Sincere head pastors do not with any malice reject others with pastors' hearts. The head pastors just cannot conceive of how it all could work together. It is usually their heart to protect their own flocks that motivates the head pastors to stop others from dividing the sheep. The problems we have described do not result from evil hearts. These problems are primarily the outcome of an unscriptural wineskin — one without all the anointings functioning together.

We need the higher anointings. God's greater works require His greater gifts. The original apostles in the book of Acts were accused of "turning the world upside down." Would twelve men with the anointing of pastor have had such an impact? Hardly! Why didn't God choose a teacher to send to Nineveh instead of the prophet Jonah? Because a teacher wouldn't have had a chance at bringing a city to its knees! If Philip had been like the average tongues-speaking Christian today, do you think Samaria would have been shaken in a few days (Acts 8:4-8)? Of course not! Is there a pastor in America who could have filled the shoes of John the Baptist? Not without receiving a prophetic anointing. Send one of our seminary graduates to Africa, and he or she may learn the language this year, win a dozen natives next year, and in a few years possibly have a church of about two hundred people. Instead, let's send an apostle like John G. Lake, who in the early part of the twentieth century was responsible for thousands of souls being saved in Africa. If we were to study the moves of God in history, we would see how God always used leaders anointed as apostles and prophets. Those are the anointings that we need in church leadership today. We won't have God's power without them.

It would be impossible for God to pour the new wine of His Holy Spirit into our present-day church structures. God doesn't do it because it would be disastrous: everything would rip! It would be like trying to pour a bathtub full of water into a cup; you just cannot do it. So long as we hold to the present structure of the church, limiting ourselves to the ministries of pastors and administrators and clinging to our traditional concepts of how the church leaders are to function, there can be no mighty awakening in our midst. Our wineskins cannot hold the new wine.

CHAPTER 21

THE WHOLE CHURCH

Imagine a New Testament church in your area. First, picture an apostle with a direct commission from Jesus to establish a work in your city. That apostle would have the anointing to draw together a team of prophets, teachers, those with gifts of miracles and healing, helps ministers, administrators, and tongues-speaking prayer warriors. Envision those elders gathered together on a regular basis, seeking the Lord, ministering to Him, and receiving direction (Acts 13:1-3).

Now place five evangelists working among the high schoolers, and five more among the grade-school children. Send out anointed evangelists to reach your city through radio and television; allow them to share the Gospel under the leading of the Holy Spirit with every home in your city once or twice each year. Place five or more evangelists working among the senior citizens in the rest homes and community centers.

Now choose pastors with true hearts for God's people. Do not burden them with building programs or financial concerns, but send them out to visit the lame, the blind, the imprisoned, the orphan, and the widow. Commission an army of shepherds to invite straying Christians over for dinner, to minister to their families, and to draw them out of the world.

Assign fifty pastors who have hearts for the children to telephone those children and visit them in their homes. Let others care for the older saints, loving them and watching over their personal needs. Have twenty or thirty pastors open their homes to gather in the lost sheep. And bring them all into the house of God where the apostles, prophets, and teachers can equip and strengthen them.

Allow those with gifts of healing and miracles to lay hands on the lost sheep and their children. Instruct these ministers to visit the hospitals regularly and to build a reputation whereby the hospital staff respect and look forward to their coming. Release the administrators to handle the finances, construct a beautiful temple for the glory of God, and organize the saints so that outreaches, food distribution, social gatherings, and other activities are completed with harmony and grace. Put into office the deacons who are filled with the Spirit of God, and let them serve so that those with the higher anointings are free to devote themselves to prayer and ministry of the Word. Take the chains and traditional restrictions off the church, and let the believers minister in their anointings.

How much of an impact do you think that church would have on your city? Think about it, and let hope rise in your heart.

CHAPTER 22

UNDERSTANDING
THE ANOINTINGS

Before we discuss the practical aspects of the new wineskin, we need to understand some additional truths about the anointings. Let's remember that the word *anointing* refers to a special act of God's Spirit coming upon and transforming a person. Not only does the person's heart change, but other characteristics also are molded supernaturally, enabling that person to carry out the ministry.

It is important to see how a person's thought patterns change when he or she becomes anointed. This is most obvious in the Old Testament, where we see leaders one day being ordinary people (especially shepherds) and the next day powerful leaders. When the Spirit brings an anointing, He transforms the person's mind.

As we study the various gifts, we discover that each one has *a certain way of thinking* associated with it. For example, pastors think primarily about the welfare of their people. Administrators think in terms of progress, organization, and efficiency. Teachers are constantly concerned with imparting truth. And prophets all have certain thought patterns and ways of dealing with situations that are related to the messages on their hearts. Each anointing has characteristic ways of thinking that have been designed by the Holy Spirit.

Let's look at the various gifts in operation. If several children were to sneak into a church sanctuary with marking pens and make marks all over the walls, different people would respond differently. Upon discovering the problem, a pastor probably first would call in the parents and the children for counseling. The administrator immediately would telephone the church treasurer to see if there were enough money for paint, and then would assign three hard workers to do the job. A teacher may want to present a series of lessons to the congregation on how to raise a family according to the Bible. The prophet may fall face downward and cry out to God to help all the children in the world (or may grab hold of those children and cast devils out of them!). The apostle probably would disciple the little ones into becoming full-time evangelists.

Notice that each person perceives the problem differently: the pastor may see the problem in the child/parent relationships, while the administrator sees the problem on the wall of the sanctuary, and the prophet identifies Satan's activity in this world. Therefore, everyone has a different solution. In our example here, I do not want to stereotype, but I do hope you recognize the different ways of thinking. With new thought patterns comes supernatural understanding.

The apostle John explained this to us:

> "And as for you, the anointing which you
> received from Him abides in you, and you

have no need for anyone to teach you; but as *His anointing teaches you* about all things, and is true and is not a lie, and just as it has taught you, you abide in Him" (1 John 2:27, italics added).

An anointing opens a person's eyes to see and understand whatever is needed for a specific ministry.

I like to compare an anointing to a flashlight; the light can reveal things in the dark that you otherwise could not see. God's act of setting up certain ways of thinking within people's minds allows them to look at life in a unique way and to perceive God's answers to problems.

Notice that "His anointing teaches you." The supernatural understanding does not come as a separate voice from heaven or from somewhere else outside the person. Direction comes from the anointing *within*. When you are anointed, you supernaturally know what you are supposed to do. You are not able to explain how you know certain things; you just know them in your spirit. That is the guidance of an anointing.

For example, anointed pastors *do not need to be taught* how to speak to their sheep in ways that make the sheep feel secure and accepted; warmth, love and the appropriate words flow out of the spirits of pastors without any effort. Likewise evangelists, *by divine inspiration*, know the right words to say to an unsaved person and how to motivate that person to respond to the Gospel. Administrators *instinctively (or spiritually)* know how to delegate responsibility, and easily can see how things should be organized so that they will run effectively. Those with healing or

115

miracles ministries *spontaneously* know the right words to say or the actions to take in order to create faith and break the bondages that keep people from receiving a healing or a miracle. Apostles are *guided by the Spirit* to fulfill the visions God has given them.

Divine guidance does not negate the need for human guidance. In the area of your anointing, "you have no need for anyone to teach you" (1 John 2:27). Pastors do not need training in how to pastor, but they may need to be taught how to understand God's Word, how to administrate, and how to evangelize. Evangelists do not need to learn from another human how to lead someone to Jesus, but they may need someone to teach them how to handle money, how to manage their homes, or how to publish books. Those anointed to minister to young children do not need teaching on how to speak to children, but they may need help in setting up a program or organizing workers. Anointed teachers learn directly from God how to present Bible truths in ways that set people free, but they may need human guidance in learning how to love their children. We all need training in many areas of our lives, but in the areas of our anointings, our guidance comes from the Holy Spirit.

Another truth about anointings is that when the Holy Spirit flows through an anointed minister, *the presence of God is revealed through that person.* First Corinthians 12:7 explains that a gift is "the manifestation of the Spirit." The gifts are avenues through which the Spirit of God makes Himself known to us. When rivers of living water flow out of a person, the presence and nature of God are revealed. Or in other words, Jesus, who lives within, shows Himself outwardly. Paul wrote of this in 2 Corinthians 4:11: "that the life of Jesus also may be manifested in our mortal flesh." This divine presence was recognizable on the face of Moses (2 Cor. 3:7) and also upon Stephen as he was being stoned to death by the Jews (Acts 7:54-60). All Christians can expect to manifest the presence of God to some degree; however, an anointing opens the door for the Holy Spirit to flow out in a unique, powerful way. It is Jesus who lives within, showing Himself by the Spirit to the world.

Every person must bow in the presence of God. Therefore, *when Jesus is being revealed through an anointed person, the spirits of the people nearby yield.* For example, when Saul became anointed as king, instantly the people began looking to him for direction and leadership (1 Sam. 9:27-12:25). When the queen of Sheba perceived how God had anointed Solomon with wisdom and blessings, "there was no more spirit in her" (1 Kings 10:4-5). King David described this power when he praised God, "Who subdues my people under me" (Psalm 144:2). No Christian should bow to another human being. However, there is a real and active force that flows out of an anointed individual, and those who yield to it are bowing inwardly to the very presence of God.

Let's look at an example that will make this submission to God's presence more recognizable. If you have been in a church where tongues and interpretations of tongues are common, then you probably have observed this. When a person in the midst of a congregation speaks out a message in tongues, one of two reactions usually occurs among the Christians present. If the message truly is anointed by the Holy Spirit, then the spirits of the Christians listening yield to it; as soon as the person speaks out, everyone's attention is drawn supernaturally to receive. It is as if the Holy Spirit flowing through the speaker pulls on the hearts of all the believers, causing them to sense His presence. If the person speaking is not anointed, then a different reaction occurs: maybe only a few sitting close by will respond, or the spirits of those who are mature in the Lord will reject the message. What we need to recognize is that an anointing from God has a noticeable, supernatural effect upon those present.

Another example will help clarify this submission to God's presence, as well as shed more light on the administrator's anointing. Administrators are leaders or governors over the various ministries in the Body of Christ. God empowers each administrator with supernatural wisdom in how to organize and delegate; God also anoints each one with His presence, which causes others to follow the administrator's instructions. I know one brother who can give directions and everyone listening immediately will snap into action and obey. Why does everyone obey him when someone else could give the very same directions and there would be little response? It is the administrative anointing.

We must not confuse an organizer with an administrator. An administrator is someone who has God-given influence to guide, direct, and delegate responsibilities. An organizer may be a deacon or a servant without an administrative anointing. With God's anointing comes the flow of the Holy Spirit, which causes others to yield.

Each anointing results in a different form of submission. The anointing upon pastors causes the sheep to hear their voices and to be drawn supernaturally to them (John 10:4-5; 14-16). For teachers, the Holy Spirit opens the ears of their hearers to understand; under that anointing, it is as if the listeners are eagerly sitting at the feet of those teachers. Those truly anointed for miracles or gifts of healings have the Holy Spirit working with them so that thoughts of sickness and disease are broken forcefully in the minds and hearts of those receiving ministry. When those anointed for miracles say, "Be healed!" any resisting doubts yield supernaturally. The presence of God upon prophets causes people to humble themselves, redirect their lives, and submit to the authoritative words the prophets speak. In the lives of apostles, the spirits of pastors, teachers, evangelists, administrators, and all the church bow. Through the anointings, our Lord reveals Himself and causes people to yield in various ways.

Let's summarize these truths about anointings:

1. When a person receives an anointing from the Holy Spirit, his or her thought patterns undergo a transformation in ways that enable that person to carry out a particular ministry.

2. An anointed person receives guidance and wisdom from the Holy Spirit in the area of his or her anointing.

3. An anointing allows the Holy Spirit to flow out of a person and manifest the presence of God for a specific ministry.

4. Each anointing produces a unique submission in the hearts of those receiving ministry.

Having looked at these recognizable characteristics of any anointing, we now are ready to see how the church must be reorganized in many practical ways, so that powerful, fruitful ministry can result.

CHAPTER 23

ORGANIZING
THE CHURCH

Now let's try to think like God thinks. When we look at the church to see who should do what, we must not look at education or experience. We must focus instead on God's anointings. *The church must be organized around the anointings.* The person you want to be in charge of a specific ministry is the one who has:

1. divinely inspired thought patterns,

2. supernatural guidance,

3. the presence of God manifesting, and

4. the submission of others to follow him or her.

Who should preach at a church or teach at a Bible study? It should be the leader who is anointed to preach or teach at the time. Obviously, this is different from our traditional understanding. Usually the pastor is left with the job of speaking, but that is many times a drastic mistake, and it grieves the Holy Spirit. Some of the most powerful moves of the Spirit in history were run with an openness among leaders such that they waited on God before services to see who should bring the message. Of course, there is nothing wrong with having a minister who does most of the preaching, but there always should be a willingness to yield to God at a moment's notice.

On one occasion, I visited a church in another town, not knowing a single person in the building (other than my wife, who was with me). The minister, who in no way even was acquainted with me, pointed to me as I sat in the congregation and announced that God wanted me to preach. That evening, I experienced one of the most powerful anointings to preach I ever have had! Conversely, when I pastored a church for several years, there were times when I knew the anointing was not on me to preach, but I preached anyway because I had been taught that *it was my job*. I now know both sides of this issue, and I believe we must break free of our traditional thinking. The Holy Spirit chooses the person He wants to preach by anointing that person. A Spirit-led church will move with the Spirit.

What about leadership of the other ministries? Who should oversee the youth? Children's ministries? Finances? Ushers? Worship? It is obvious: God's choice is identified by the anointing. Look at the heart, the "way of thinking." Through whom does the presence of God manifest so that others follow? The person who is burdened with the needs of youth is the one whom the Spirit is anointing. Whoever is most concerned that the church be a financial success is God's choice for the financial oversight. An usher sent from God is the mature believer who arrives at the church early and greets people with enthusiasm. An anointed worship leader is the person who feels miserable after church for a whole day if the worship service was not excellent. A teacher is the one concerned about the lack of teaching, and who repeatedly complains about how little of the Bible people are receiving. God's administrator is the Christian who is frustrated with how unorganized and inefficient things are. (I learned a long time ago that people who complain a lot are very often leaders who have not been given an opportunity to serve.) The children's minister is the one who cries for the little ones and who the children supernaturally look to for direction.

An anointed person usually considers his or her ministry the most important one. For example, an anointed secretary thinks he or she is keeping the whole church operating (and that may be true). An anointed nursery director considers the nursery to be more important than any other ministry. Such ways of thinking are marks of God's anointing.

Do you want to know who God's choice is? Then look at the heart that is burdened and seeks for a solution. Watch the person who is motivated to spend extra time and pay the price to get the best results. Watch the eyes of the congregation and see who they look to for direction. Their spirits and yours will recognize God's anointing.

Most churches are not run by this principle. Usually when someone is needed to teach the children, the position is offered to "whoever is willing" at that time; the one who accepts is usually the dear brother or sister who wants to help, but only because there is a need. This creates a church that is based on *needs* rather than on *anointings*. Or, we put into a position the person with some past experience, training, or worldly knowledge. An assortment of leaders are then in charge, but the Spirit flows through them to only a limited degree.

I have come to the conclusion that no work is better than a "dead" work. If the only children's teacher is serving out of duty rather than out of the Holy Spirit's anointing, then the church is better off without the ministry. If such a teacher gets up in front of the children Sunday after Sunday, those children are learning, above, all else, that the Christian life is boring and burdensome. If no life is flowing out of the worship leader, then a church is better off without worship. "Something" is not always better than nothing.

We must grasp this truth: that Jesus is the Head of the Church. It is His job to provide anointed teachers, leaders, administrators, and other ministers. It is our job simply to recognize the need and to ask Him to supply the resources. The Spirit always places people where He wants them. If we try to place an unanointed person in a position of ministry, then we are working against the Holy Spirit. I have found that when I stop a dead ministry and wait on God, in a very short time the Spirit raises up a new leader for that ministry. If, however, I try to keep a dead ministry going, and allow the unanointed leader to labor on, then the dead work also labors on and on and on — becoming noticeably stinky, spreading death to other parts of the Body, and never allowing room for the life-giving vision and plan ordained by the Head of the Church. There's only one thing to do with a dead work: Bury it!

I am not ignoring the need for Christian maturity, training, encouragement, and experience. Maturity is vital, and we always must take it into account before recognizing anointed individuals. Training, encouragement, and experience are important too; however, they are secondary in organizing a ministry. It is the anointing of God on which we must focus.

God's choice for a ministry is identified by His anointing. We must not depend on education, qualifications, experience, age, or any other natural characteristic. Instead we must pray and watch, keeping in mind these characteristics of an anointed person:

1. One who loves God and serves Him faithfully,

2. One whose heart is burdened for a particular ministry need,

3. One who manifests the presence of Jesus within that area of ministry,

4. One to whom others willingly yield.

As we have seen, that anointed person will have supernatural guidance concerning how the specific ministry is to function. Why would you choose anyone whom God has not chosen? If no one can be found, then we must "bury" that ministry until the Holy Spirit finds someone. It is simple to organize the church when we see as God sees.

CHAPTER 24

MEETINGS AND GATHERINGS

Most churches today follow a standardized program at nearly all their meetings. Protestant churches typically open with a prayer and a word of welcome, then they have singing and the offering, followed by announcements, sometimes communion, then a sermon, and finally a closing song and prayer. Even in Pentecostal churches, which lay claim to "freedom in the Spirit," there is usually a set time between the worship and the sermon when the Spirit is allowed to work through His gifts. Other meetings are similarly prestructured, and the agenda is fairly predictable. Whether or not we like to admit it, our religious traditions are well-established.

Such uniformity is not seen in the New Testament. Second Corinthians 3:17 tells us: "Now the Lord is the Spirit; and where the Spirit of the Lord is, there is liberty." Jesus similarly explained, "The wind blows where it wishes and you hear the sound of it, but do not know where it comes from and where it is going; so is every one who is born of the Spirit" (John 3:8). The more that Jesus is allowed His rightful position as Lord, the more the Spirit leads in freedom. When the Spirit leads, you do not know what is going to happen next; you can recognize the leading ("hear the sound of it"), but you do not know from where it comes or where it is going. The Holy Spirit is creative and He is free from limitations.

In the New Testament we see not one but many different kinds of meetings. As we look at these, it is helpful to distinguish the large public gatherings from the smaller meetings, which met primarily in homes. In Acts 2:46 we read that the early believers were "continuing with one mind in the temple, and breaking bread from house to house." Acts 5:42 tells us that this was the common practice: "And every day, in the temple and from house to house, they kept right on teaching and preaching Jesus as the Christ." The people met in both large and small settings.

Let's look at some of those meetings so we can understand better how the Spirit may be released to act with greater freedom in our midst today. Large gatherings recorded in the book of Acts include the following:

> The one on Pentecost day, when Peter speaks to several thousand (Acts 2:1-41)
>
> The daily ongoing temple gatherings (2:46; 5:42)
>
> The times Peter and John preach to multitudes on the portico of Solomon (3:11; 5:12)
>
> The time in which the building where the believers are meeting is shaken by the power of God (4:31)
>
> The many meetings on the streets (5:14-16)
>
> Gatherings in the temple, when the apostles teach (5:18-21)

The large congregational meeting in which the disciples choose deacons to wait on tables (6:1-6)

Open meetings in Samaria and "all the cities," in which Philip preaches to the multitudes (8:4-8, 40)

The gathering of Samaritan believers, in which Peter and John pray for them to be baptized in the Holy Spirit (8:14-17)

Gatherings throughout the Samaritan villages, in which Peter, John, and Philip preach (8:25)

Gatherings in Antioch, in which Barnabas, Paul, and others preach (11:20-26)

Other gatherings in Antioch, in which Agabus and the other prophets speak out (11:27-28)

Gatherings in the synagogues, in which Paul, and sometimes Barnabas or Silas, preach (13:5, 14; 14:1; 17:1-2; 17:10, 17: 18:4, 19; 19:8)

Gatherings in outdoor public places (13:44; 14:8-18; 17:17, 19-34; 27:33-37), and wherever else the church could gather (14:27)

Public meetings in which Apollos refutes the Jews (18:28)

Some of these references imply that many similar large gatherings were going on continually. The others describe individual meetings.

Notice that although nearly all of these larger meetings mention an apostle at the forefront, the spokesmen at other meetings include Stephen (the deacon), Philip (the evangelist), and prophets, such as Agabus. Some of these gatherings were open to the public, with both believers and unbelievers present. Some were evangelistic in nature, while others were for the saints to receive teaching or to pray.

At the same time, smaller group meetings, especially those that took place in homes, are recorded in the book of Acts. These were the settings for prayer (12:12), the breaking of bread (2:46; 20:7-12), fellowship (2:46), teaching and exhorting (10:24-48; 16:14-15, 32, 30; 18:7; 28:30-31), the working of miracles (20:7-12; 9:39), and the ministering of prophets (21:8-14). In these smaller groups both the leaders and the rest of the saints were able to minister and receive ministry.

Further light is shown on the early believers' meetings by reading Paul's instructions to the Corinthians:

> When you assemble, each one has a psalm, has a teaching, has a revelation, has a tongue, has an interpretation (I Cor. 14:26).

This exhortation shows us how the saints all should have an opportunity to use their gifts. This was not the pattern seen in the book of Acts when an apostle, prophet, teacher, or evangelist spoke to a large crowd; however, it appears to have been a common practice, at least in the Corinthian church.

This is not to say that every meeting of believers should be simply for the purpose of everyone functioning in the spiritual gifts. Three chapters earlier Paul writes about a believers' meeting in which the Lord's Supper is central (1 Cor. 11:18-34). In Acts 20:7-12 we read about a gathering in an upper room, where saints come together to break bread, but then Paul teaches from the Word of God for many hours afterward. Several believers' meetings in the book of Acts focused on prayer or on one person teaching. There was no set program.

God wants His Church to have all forms of ministry. We need group prayer, teaching, fellowship, the breaking of bread together, and opportunities for all Christians present to function in the spiritual gifts. We also need large gatherings, in which the apostles, prophets, teachers, evangelists, and those with miracles and healing ministries can exercise their gifts. We need times when only believers are gathered and other times that are open to all.

The most common large gatherings recorded in the New Testament were led by an apostle. From the phrase "when you assemble" (1 Cor. 14:26), we can conclude that the most common smaller group meeting, at least in Corinth, allowed all the saints to bring forth what God was putting on their hearts. Acts 20:7 tells us that the Lord's Supper also was celebrated very frequently. And, of course, prayer meetings must have been common, too.

To be able to accept such variety in the meetings that we see in the New Testament, we must break free of the traditional idea that each gathering must be run by a single minister. We must no longer limit ourselves or the Holy Spirit to the pastor/congregation setup. In the meetings I have called "believers' meetings," any believer could minister, but at other small gatherings we see different ministry gifts at the forefront. The apostles often ministered and taught in the homes. Agabus, the prophet, was ministering in the home group described in Acts 21:8-11. Paul, before he received his apostolic anointing (Acts 13:1-3), had a group of disciples under him; so then we see Paul as a prophet and teacher leading those disciples. The seven deacons oversaw the gatherings in which the widows were served food daily (Acts 6:1-6). First Timothy 5:17 refers to elders who work hard at preaching and teaching. The Holy Spirit was not restricted by any one design of a flock being under a person anointed as "pastor." Therefore, we cannot confine our thinking either.

Nor can we limit the meeting times. Today, Christians tend to think of Sunday mornings and Wednesday evenings as the appropriate occasions for church meetings. Without realizing it, we begin to program our minds and lives to these man-made traditions. Who said Christians should gather together on Sunday mornings? In recent years much of the Spirit's activity has been outside the accepted meeting times. God has blessed home Bible studies, prayer breakfasts, conferences, college organizations, The Full Gospel Business Men's Fellowship, and so on, which have broken the traditional framework of meeting on Sundays. The Holy Spirit will not be restricted to our time-scheduled wineskin.

Nowhere in the Bible are we told to gather together on Sunday mornings. We are exhorted to be led by the Spirit. We must have fellowship with other Christians, but I do not believe God considers sitting in a pew fellowship. True fellowship involves deep, intimate, open relationships with other believers. We need home meetings, prayer meetings, the breaking of bread together, and opportunities to use our individual gifts. We need church several times a day! In addition, we must have times to gather for teaching, preaching, and ministry under those with God's higher anointings. But God has not limited Himself, or us, to Sunday morning services.

Finally, we cannot restrict our thinking as to what constitutes the Church. The Church is wherever two or more Christians are gathered together. Two or three believers fellowshipping at the restaurant in the name of Jesus are just as much a church as those who gather in a building on Sunday mornings. What the young person with an evangelistic anointing does on the street Saturday night is just as important to the Body as what goes on inside the church building. The Church is the people of God doing the work of God. A person with a pastor's heart who gathers new believers into his or her home for dinner and fellowship is just as much a part of the Body as the minister who counsels people. A father bringing his family together for devotions is "having church." The Church is the people, and the Church's meetings are where God's people meet — on the street, in a restaurant, in a home, or in a building.

We must break free of our man-made traditions so that we can receive the new wine about to be poured out. If we cling to established meeting times, structures, places, or programs, we will not be able to cooperate with the Spirit of God. The great outpouring of God's Spirit to come will be poured only into a new, fuller wineskin.

Do not think that I am teaching against Sunday services, church buildings, or pastor-run groups. I am not. I merely am trying to shake you, to challenge you, and to wake you to a much bigger picture of the Body of Christ. We may always have Sunday morning services, buildings, pastor-led fellowships and administrator-run groups, but we are going to see much, much more as the Spirit of God pours forth upon us. A new wineskin is forming. Let's not allow man-made religious traditions to keep us from entering into it.

In no way am I implying that everyone should independently do what is right in their own eyes. On the contrary, when Christians begin to individually follow the Holy Spirit, they will be brought into the Body, not separated from it. Paul explains that it is the Spirit that baptizes or submerges us into the Body (1 Cor. 12:13). The more that people individually yield to the Holy Spirit, the more they are moved into their God-ordained positions in the Church. The Body is being fitly framed together by the Spirit (Eph. 2:21-22).

The form taking shape will not have the structure that the present-day churches have. It will not be organized around denominations or doctrines. Each person who follows the Holy Spirit will be supernaturally guided into position with the rest of the saints. In that transition, in which the saints are molded together, the overall structure of the Church will take shape as God intends. Those He has appointed as leaders will emerge as leaders. Apostles, prophets, and teachers will move to the forefront. Individual Christians will do "the work of service" (Eph. 4:12). Those saints who gather others into their homes for fellowship earnestly will want the oversight of an apostle. The small groups coming together for teaching and the breaking of bread will recognize those whom God has sent to oversee. The prophets will have tangible anointings upon their lives, and the Spirit of God will cause them to go where they are needed. The evangelists active on the street will work to further the overall ministry of the whole Church. When the elders call a meeting for all the saints in a region, the saints will gather together, bringing their individual ministries into proper relationship with the leaders.

Supernaturally, we will be made one. Existing denominations or legal corporations neither will tie us together, nor divide us. Neither will agreements written on paper or financial dependencies cause the Body to be one. Organizations will continue, yet they will not be the binding force — for the Spirit of God through His anointings will accomplish this coming unity.

How? Let's discuss it more fully in the remaining chapters.

CHAPTER 25

UNITY IN THE BODY OF CHRIST

The greatest challenge of the Body of Christ is the operation of all the gifts in unity. How can a thousand different meetings being held throughout a city be united as a single Body? How can leaders who think differently work together? How can a prophet who is radical, assertive, and spiritually oriented work along-side a teacher who is logical, consistent, and well-balanced? How can an aggressive, energetic evangelist tolerate a pastor who is willing to work patiently with the same group of believers year after year? How can finances be distributed when every leader thinks his or her ministry is the most important? And how can an apostle who is compelled with a vision from God be in harmony with administrators who desire growth in a slow, progressive, and efficient manner? Then what about the healing ministers who, in the eyes of the administrators, are wasting their lives praying instead of working and producing? Can such a mixture of giftings walk hand-in-hand?

In 1 Corinthians 12 Paul deals with several issues relating to the unity of the Body. Let's identify these, because only if we understand and apply them, will the New Testament wineskin work in today's world.

First, Paul explains that there are many parts to the Body and that God is the One who places each

137

part where He desires (12:12-18). We are told that every member is essential: A foot cannot say to an ear, "I have no need of you." A natural body without an eye is handicapped. So, also, the Body of Christ without prophets, without evangelists, or without any one of its other members, is incomplete. The first truth we need to accept is that every part is necessary. The senior minister needs to welcome the evangelists. Every Christian must release the administrators to organize, plan, and delegate. We all need to look at the prophet and say, "I need you." *The first step toward unity is the realization that we all need each other and that we must release each other for ministry.*

This implies that Christians must overcome the tendency to control and judge brothers and sisters who are not like themselves. I have learned as a father that my family runs smoothly if I can keep the children from trying to correct each other; if my older son is not concerned with keeping his younger sister in line, and if my daughter will leave my younger boy alone, everything stays in harmony. It is the same way in the Church. If we can train Christians to "mind their own business," then the Body will function.

Now I am not saying that we allow people to backslide or to get involved in sin. Those things need our attention. However, *the tendency to try to govern other people's "ways of ministry" must be defeated.* When we judge each other, we judge God (James 4:11).

The key to working in harmony is *trust*: Trust the Holy Spirit that He knows how to work through people in different ways. Trust God, for He has placed the members where He chooses (1 Cor. 12:18). Trust

Jesus, who is the Head and who is able to correct those in error. And trust each other, that we each can be led by the Spirit of God.

Another truth that Paul imparts concerning the unity of the Body is that we must honor the *lesser gifts*. The higher gifts normally attract the attention of other people, but Paul explains that the lesser gifts are the most essential ones (1 Cor. 12:20-25), and they are the ones that God wants us to honor. Eyes and hands are very important to us, but in truth, they are the least valuable parts of our natural bodies; for we could live without eyes and hands, but we never could survive without a liver, or intestines, or any other part about which we seldom think. In the same way, evangelists are more important than prophets, for people need salvation more than they need direction. Most people need to see pastors more than they need to see a miracle. The prayer warriors who pray in tongues are more necessary for the health of the Body than a teacher is. Administrators and pastors are more important than apostles, prophets, or teachers,

HIGHER GIFTS

| Apostle |
| Prophet |
| Teacher |
| Miracles |
| Healings |
| Helps |
| Administration |
| Tongues |
| Pastor |
| Evangelist |

GREATER IMPORTANCE

since without the work of the administrators and pastors, there would be no group of believers to exhort or direct. This interdependence creates respect for the lesser gifts, and thus establishes the proper order and unity.

The higher gifts exist for the lower gifts. Apostles must give their lives for the strengthening of pastors and evangelists. Pastors must lay down their lives for their sheep. Evangelists give themselves to the world. Administrators must direct their ministries to the saints "below" them. And prophets and teachers exist for the lesser gifts. This gives us a picture of how the ministers with the higher anointings are to direct their ministries toward the ministers below them — not to rule over them, but to pour out their lives for them.

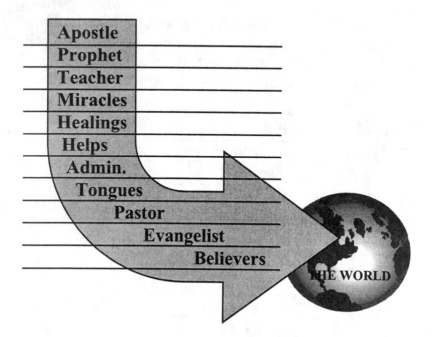

Too often this direction of flow is reversed in the church. Pastors do not need to be invited over to everyone's house so that the people can minister to them; pastors should be strong enough in God so that they can bring people into *their* homes and minister to *them*. The teachers must not spend their time straightening out the prophets; they must dedicate their efforts to teaching the people. When the administrators try to slow down the apostle, they are out of place, for it is not their job to work on the apostle, but to organize the people so that the apostle's vision will be fulfilled. Whenever the direction of flow is reversed, problems result and the church is out of order. This does not mean that the prophets cannot confront the apostle, or that the teacher cannot instruct the prophet, but the primary focus of each ministry must be toward those with lesser gifts.

This direction of flow is related to the order that God has established in his Church (1 Cor. 12:28). In the next chapter we will discuss more specifically this order and the authority associated with it. After that, we will look at the final but most important ingredient for the whole Church to function in unity.

CHAPTER 26

THE AUTHORITY OF THE HIGHER GIFTS

And God has appointed in the church, first apostles, second prophets, third teachers, then miracles, then gifts of healings, helps, administrations, various kinds of tongues (1 Cor. 12:28).

Unless a church recognizes God's order of authority, the Body will never function in harmony with all the anointings working together.

The higher gifts are not only *appointed* for authority; they are also *anointed for it*. A person who has a higher gift has a "higher" way of thinking. That person's thought patterns and heart are designed by God for leadership. Just as in the Old Testament we see common shepherds instantaneously becoming great leaders by the anointing of God, so also the anointings enable us to exercise authority properly. When we say that a person who has a higher gift has a higher way of thinking, we are not implying that the person has a better or holier way of thinking. Rather, the gift simply allows the person to see things from a broader perspective and with a heightened awareness. This way of thinking can be illustrated by an army in which the sergeant on the front lines with his men has

143

a perspective different from that of the general who has the battle strategy and who gives the orders from behind the lines. It is the apostle who has the overall vision from God, and the apostle bases all decisions on the fulfillment of that vision. In contrast, a pastor (who we will compare with the sergeant in our illustration) thinks primarily of what is good for his or her own people.

As we study each of the gifts, we discover that the higher the gift, the more in touch the anointed person is with God's direction; the lower the gift, the more aware the person is of the people's needs and the natural consequences. Apostles are aware continually of whether or not the overall vision is being furthered. Prophets are concerned primarily that God's specific directives are being followed. Teachers evaluate everything in terms of biblical accuracy. Miracle ministers are more spiritually sensitive to God's power than are the healing ministers, who desire to see God's hand gently work among the people. Administrators think of practical and natural consequences. Pastors focus on the welfare of their sheep, and evangelists

ANOINTING	FOCUSED ON
Apostle	God's Commission
Prophet	God's Directives
Teacher	God's Written Truth
Miracles	God's Power
Healings	God's Love and Healing
Helps	The Apostle's Directives
Administration	Practical Programs and Goals
Tongues	Areas of Prayer Need
Pastor	Needs of the Congregation
Evangelist	The Unsaved World

are always concerned about the lost masses. Each of these ways of thinking is needed, but the higher ways are more suited for the higher positions of authority over the church.

Let's consider an example involving an apostle, an administrator, and a pastor. If the apostle senses God's leading to construct a church building, the minister serving with him will judge the project differently. The administrator will evaluate the project to see if it is practical and financially feasible. The pastor will consider whether the congregation would be overly burdened by the financial pressure. The pastor's and administrator's ways of thinking are not bad or wrong; they are simply "lower," and they were never meant to be in the rulership position. The anointed apostle will base his decision (after talking to the administrator, pastor, and others) on God's commission, regardless of financial impossibility or the effect on the people. In his higher way of thinking, obedience to God overrules logic and personal needs. Of course, the average pastor or administrator who desires to please God would agree that God's leading is the most important factor, but in practice the pastor and the administrator have a very difficult time "hearing" God's leading over the threat to the sheep or the impossibility of finances. With an apostle's vision comes supernatural faith that enables him to see beyond need or people's feelings. Because of this, the apostle's anointing must be respected and given sway.

God's order means life or death to the church. If we put a pastor into the authority position it is almost, if not totally, impossible for the church to minister to more than fifty people. As we saw earlier, if an administrator takes control of a congregation or denomination, thus replacing an apostle, that group may grow in size, but it will establish its wineskin, become inflexible, and then die spiritually. Administrators like to design and implement programs, and that is a necessary function, but they are seventh in the line of authority, and their programs are supposed to be "ripped up" or altered regularly by those with higher anointings so that the wineskin will be stretched continually. A church run by an evangelist typically has rapid growth at first, but quickly ends in disaster, with great financial difficulties. Most prophet-led groups are radical and committed, but short-lived and off-balanced. Churches headed by a miracles and healings minister are unstable and often doctrinally unsound. Teacher-led groups are consistent and stable, but tend to be impersonal, and they soon stagnate.

Just as disastrous as putting a person with the wrong anointing in charge is the forcing of a higher anointing under a lower anointing. To put an administrator under a pastor will leave that administrator in frustration. To place a prophet under an administrator is to prepare for war. To place any higher gift under a lower gift is to grieve the Holy Spirit. Any person with a higher calling who submits to someone with a lower gift will be bored and frustrated. Every time we change God's order, the church suffers.

In making these statements I am not referring to submission in every area of a person's life. All Christians must respect the other anointings. A prophet sometimes needs to be ministered to by a pastor, and a teacher may go to a person with a healing ministry for prayer. Those with the higher gifts must submit to those with the lower gifts, because the lower gifts are needed for personal ministry. However, the overall operation of the church must be run in God's order of the higher gifts being over the lower ones.

There is a God-ordained order of authority. God appointed it. *Now is the time for the Church to accept the wisdom of God.*

In speaking of authority in the local church, I am not implying a strict or "lording-it-over" relationship. Those in authority are to rule with hearts of humility and love. Unity in the Spirit must be sought by all. The relationship should be much like the marriage relationship, in which the husband is head of the wife, but must lead with love and understanding. It is important to remember also that God can speak through any Christian, no matter how young or old. Every leader must be sensitive to how the Holy Spirit can use any member of the congregation. When elders are servants, leadership is not bondage, but a welcomed blessing. Authority in the Christian context does not imply a master-servant relationship.

However, the authority and submission relationship is real. There are several exhortations in the New Testament to submit to one's spiritual leaders. Some Christians have a hard time accepting any hierarchy in church government; they reason that we are all brothers and sisters in the Lord. Everyone recognizes a chain of command on their jobs, in schools, in the military, and even on the football field, but when we talk about the church context, some Christians rebel. It is true that all Christians are priests unto God and that everyone should sense the Spirit's leading for the decisions in their own lives. But God does have a system of rulership for the Church. Even in our physical bodies, there are parts that give directions and other parts that "obey." In the same way, the Body of Christ can function only as the proper authority and submission relationships are exercised.

We already have discussed the position of authority that the elders are to hold over each church. Now let's see how these elders are supposed to arrive at decisions and oversee the congregation. Most churches today have ignored God's plan and have substituted decision-making policies, much like secular organizations, businesses, or clubs. Let's look at each of the popular forms of government within today's churches and see why they are wrong for the Body of Christ.

In some churches the leaders (or board members or ruling body — whatever name they are given) vote on different issues, and the majority or two-thirds of the group rules. Unfortunately, division and controversy is inevitable, because people must take sides. In addition, there is no guarantee that the majority is correct when it comes to spiritual issues. Many times in the Scriptures, God had to raise up one or several leaders to stand against the majority. Furthermore, we know that voting is not God's plan for the Church, because nowhere in the Bible can we find Christians trying to settle issues by this means.

Another form of government among elders is based on the philosophy that discussion eventually culminates in right decision-making. The leaders in these churches discuss every topic until they can solve each problem. This system at first glance may sound right and even godly, but in practice, *discussion does not always reveal God's best.* The Jewish leaders strongly believed in this style of decision-making, and we easily can identify today the great errors they made — such as crucifying our Lord. Discussion tends to develop and bring out human ideas rather than the mind of God. *Decisions end up being based on what is practical, efficient, and financially feasible — in other words, administrative thinking.* Many churches are ruled by this lower way of thinking. Furthermore, in a church run by this principle, the person with the strongest personality dominates the conversation or summarizes most discussions in a way that sways the decisions without the others even being aware that this is occurring. We know from experience that the individuals who are the most assertive are not always right. In practice, *discussion-ruled churches tend to be administrative, one-man-ruled churches.*

A third form of decision-making that has been tried in many different churches is one in which nothing is done until all the elders are in total agreement. Discussion is incorporated, but there is more sensitivity to spiritual insight and every person's thoughts. This is an improvement over other styles, but it still opens the door for a serious problem. If everyone has to be in agreement, what happens when any one person backslides, is carnal, or simply decides to do his or her own thing? Do you delay the work of God for months? For years? Even a greater danger than waiting is the control that moves into the hands of whomever is the most fearful or the laziest. You see, all one has to do to stop any work is to say, "No." The people who most often will say "No" are those with the least amount of faith. As a consequence, the all-in-agreement church stagnates over many issues.

As I say this, do not think I am against discussion or unanimous agreement among the elders. Of course not. We must work for unity in all decisions. Every elder should bring forth insight on the various issues that face the church. Wise leaders depend upon the counsel of those who work with them. Some decisions are so crucial that only a foolish leader would proceed before all elders come into agreement. *The relationships among elders should be so loving, trusting, and gracious that the entire question of who has the authority never needs to be discussed. Perfect unity among the elders is our primary goal.*

However, we need to recognize the wisdom of God in giving us a specific order. The "whole church" will be led by an apostle who has a vision from God and hence the supernatural guidance to fulfill that vision. God's plan includes one or more prophets whose eyes are open to discern things spiritually, and who are able to rebuke those in sin and redirect the church if it veers off course. That plan also includes a team of teachers who keep the doctrine sound and the Body biblically accurate. Administrators are freed to discuss every natural problem and solution, recommending those solutions to the other elders. God's plan includes those with the ministries of miracles, healings, and helps, who can add their spiritual discernment. Finally, the prayer warriors are allowed freedom to pray through any difficulties arising, so that God's answers may be revealed, and not just man's.

God's original design was not to limit the church to voting or discussing or natural agreement. His desire is for the leaders to function *as a team, each in his or her individual anointing.* Prayer warriors can pray, administrators can evaluate and discuss, teachers may open their Bibles and present the pertinent scriptural truths, prophets may open their spirits to hear God's specific direction, and the apostle can fit everything into the overall vision. That is what we see in Acts 15:6-20, in which all the elders came together, discussed (15:6), debated (15:7), bore testimony (15:12), looked into Scripture (15:16), and allowed the apostle James to make the final ruling (15:19). That is exactly what happened in the book of Acts when the leaders of the church at Jerusalem assembled to make a decision.

Of course, this form of government leaves the final authority in the hands of an apostle. Does this scare you? Would you rather have the final authority based on a vote? Or how about basing it on discussion, which preordains that it will be an administrative decision? After observing many, many churches, I can tell you that no matter what form of government a church claims to have, there is always one person who openly or quietly holds the greatest influence over the church. Setting up the proper government is never a matter of keeping it out of the hands of one person, but putting it into the hands of God's person.

Only with God's plan are there true checks and balances. If prophets are truly of God, can there be any better check on the one in the top position? If teachers who know the Bible and administrators who are wise in the affairs of the world are both allowed to speak, can there be any wiser counsel? If prayer warriors are on their knees, why should anyone worry? If an apostle, indeed, is sent directly by God to fulfill a task, will not his Boss keep a rein on him?

Finally, in the next chapter, we will discuss the most powerful check that God has established over the leaders of His Church. It is one that guarantees that the leaders will stay in unity and never fall into sin or veer off course. It is the power that binds us together.

CHAPTER 27

MANIFESTING THE HEADSHIP OF JESUS

Churches throughout history have tried to establish unity through various human techniques. Division and strife have been a continual dilemma. Almost every denomination and Christian organization has endeavored to unite its followers around one central feature. The Roman Catholic Church has brought unity by placing all final authority in the hands of a pope. Other churches on the denominational level or the local level have similarly laid the ultimate "tie-breaker vote" in the hands of one human individual. Some look to a group of leaders to influence their work according to decisions those elders make. Others have developed unity by providing a written document such as a constitution, bylaws, or a statement of faith that serves as an anchor by which all policies and beliefs are judged. Finally, others are organized around a vision or goal, such as sending out missionaries, feeding the hungry, or winning a city for Jesus. These attempts at unity are not all wrong; we need visions, goals, leaders, and/or written documents. However, they fall short of God's solution for making people one.

The real problem is *within us*. No single person, organizational structure, doctrinal statement, or vision can solve our insufficiencies. James explains where our divisions arise: "What is the source of quarrels and conflicts among you? Is not the source your pleasures which wage war in your members?" (James 4:1). Paul similarly writes that strife comes out of the carnal, fleshly man (1 Cor. 3:1-23, Gal. 5:19-21). When we try to achieve unity based on a natural entity we are not solving the real problem, which dwells within people.

Another truth we must face is that Jesus is to be the center and focal point of the Church. He is the Head. We need to stop talking about this truth and actually see in Scripture how His headship may be realized, so that He may indeed have the final authority. If Jesus were to attend our church meetings, and we could obtain His ruling on any subject, all questions could be settled quickly. Unity must have Jesus as its center.

It is not enough to declare that the Bible is our focal point. Christians for centuries have been saying that it is our focal point, and they are still arguing and disagreeing about what the Bible means. Furthermore, the Bible does not make our decisions for us, such as when to purchase a building, how much of the finances should be sent to missions, and who is to lead our worship service. Of course, the Bible is our standard, but we need Jesus' authoritative and personal leadership coming to us directly, not through interpretations. We need not just the written Word, but the second Person of the Godhead — the Word of God Himself.

In the days just following Pentecost, Jesus did

hold the reins of the Church, and the problem of man's carnal nature was overcome. In Acts 4 we read that the early believers were "of one heart and soul" (vs. 32). They were so unified and in love that they sold their possessions and gave the proceeds to help one another. In New Testament times there were not one thousand churches in a city or one hundred different denominations. We read about "the church at Antioch" and "the church at Ephesus." These bodies of believers consisted of thousands, and yet there was a supernatural oneness. Certainly divisions developed later, but in the beginning they exercised a unity that had to have been divinely controlled by Jesus.

God speaks of this unity through the prophets in the Old Testament. In Jeremiah our Lord says, "and I will give them one heart and one way" (32:39). Imagine a congregation made up of several thousand believers all having the same purpose and desire. Notice that this oneness is established by God. He will do it. It is supernatural. Unity is a gift.

Unfortunately, most Christians have dismissed God's promises for unity, thinking that we will never actually experience it in this life. Some have concluded that it will be seen only toward the end of the world or after Jesus returns. Others have rationalized that our unity is present today, but in a mystical, unseen form. The prevailing attitude is that unity is for another time, another place, or another dimension, but is not to be shared by you and me today.

That is simply not true. God's supernatural unity and love cannot be explained away as only a spiritual bond, because the first Christians actually experienced it. Nor can we say that singleness of heart and soul is only for the beginning and end of Church history, because there were several times throughout our history when Christians in the midst of great revivals actually experienced this perfect love. This is a promise of God of which you and I actually can partake now.

The common element in every occurrence of God's divine oneness is *the manifesting presence of God.* The Jews came into unity when "the hand of God" came upon them (for example, see 2 Chron. 30:12). The early believers were bonded together when the Spirit was manifested in their midst. In history, Christians have experienced this unity during revivals in which the presence of God was sensed tangibly.

When we speak of the "manifesting presence of God," we are not referring to the state in which the Spirit of God is present everywhere at all times. We know that God is omnipresent; however, He is not *manifesting* Himself at all times everywhere. To understand the word *manifesting*, picture an angel standing before you. That angel may be there, but you could not see it or touch it. If, however, it appeared as an angel did to Peter (Acts 12:7), then you could see it with your natural eyes. When speaking of spiritual beings manifesting, we are describing how they come out of the spirit realm and make themselves known in the natural dimension.

God's Spirit manifests Himself in many ways. The Bible gives us examples in which the Spirit takes the form of a dove (Matt. 3:16), wind (Acts 2:2), fire (Acts 2:3; Exod. 24:17, 40:38), a cloud (Exod. 40:34, 1 Kings 8:10, Matt. 17:5), and light (Acts 9:3). In Exodus, when the Holy Spirit descends upon Mt. Sinai, the whole mountain quakes violently (19:18), and in Acts, when the early Christians have just finished praying together, the Spirit causes the building to shake (4:31). He also manifests Himself through the spiritual gifts (1 Cor. 12:7-10).

Notice that the people actually sense or feel God's presence. When He reveals himself at Pentecost the believers keep "feeling a sense of awe" (Acts 2:43). Several times the glory cloud of God fills the Jewish temple so forcefully that the priests cannot even stand to their feet (2 Chron. 5:13-14). In our church services today we often can sense God manifesting Himself during a very powerful worship service: a "holy hush" comes into the room, or we become aware of a tingling sensation.

These, of course, are only tiny tastes of the glory of God, but still they are evidences of His presence. In these and other ways God reveals Himself to His people.

Every time God's Spirit is manifested, supernatural "molding" power is released. When two or more people are together and the presence of God comes, their hearts and minds are being made one. The greater the manifestation, the more powerful the force to mold the people together.

Paul explains this phenomenon in 1 Corinthians 12:13: "For by one Spirit we were all baptized into one body...." Paul is not referring simply to the experience we call the baptism in the Holy Spirit. He is speaking of much more than that. The word *baptized* means "submerged." Whenever two or more believers become submerged in the Spirit together, they are fashioned into the one Body of Jesus Christ, with Him as the Head and each of them in their God-ordained positions.

James teaches us our part in this experience. Immediately after stating that our divisions stem from our own evil desires (James 4:1-3), he says that God does not manifest His Spirit in the presence of sin:

> You adulteresses, do you not know that friendship with the world is hostility toward God? Therefore whoever wishes to be a friend of the world makes himself an enemy of God. Or do you think that the Scripture speaks to no purpose: "He jealously desires the Spirit which He has made to dwell in us?" (James 4:4-5).

God protects His Spirit. He jealously watches over the Holy Spirit and will not allow His presence to be revealed when people are united to the world. James goes on to explain that the Spirit will come upon us as we turn our focus completely upon Him:

> But He gives a greater grace. Therefore it says, "God is opposed to the proud, but gives grace to the humble." Submit therefore to God. Resist the devil and he will flee from you. Draw near to God and He will draw near to you. Cleanse your hands, you sinners; and purify your hearts, you double-minded. Be miserable and mourn and weep; let your laughter be turned into mourning, and your joy to gloom. Humble yourselves in the presence of the Lord (James 4:6-10).

As we turn away from the world and from sin, and seek God, He draws near to us and the devil flees. The presence of God is then manifested.

Jesus explains it this way: "'For where two or three have gathered together in My name, there I am in their midst'" (Matt. 18:20). We must not look at this verse in the carefree manner that many Christians do. Jesus is not talking about His being present in the usual sense — that He is always present. Rather, He is telling us that wherever two or more Christians arrive at a state of total agreement (Matt. 18:18-19) — heart and soul — then His actual presence will come upon them, just as it did in the book of Acts when the believers came into one accord.

Whenever any two Christians come together and focus completely on Jesus, the presence of God is then manifested, the devil flees, all divisions disappear, and God transforms the two Christians from fleshly, carnal people into one heart and mind. There is no church problem that cannot be overcome by God's presence. There is no strife, no jealousy, no anger, and no demon that can remain in the presence of God. *It is impossible for any two Christians to disagree when they are in the manifesting presence of Jesus.* When Christians make Jesus the Head, they have no division.

The only element that can stop God's molding power is our unwillingness to focus on God. If two people come together with the goal of seeking God, but one of them is obsessed by problems and other concerns, then the presence of God will not manifest. I have observed that when everyone in a group focuses completely on Jesus, His molding power always goes into effect. However, if one person in that group refuses to turn his or her eyes to God, then that person does not experience the awesome presence of God along with the others. Any member of a group who continues to focus on things other than Jesus will be left out of His manifesting presence and His molding power.

In practice, how can this power work in the local church? When discussion, prayer, or Scripture study has not solved a disagreement among elders, they can enter into the supernatural binding force of God. If they will gather together, stop discussing, stop debating, cease all self-efforts at gaining unity, and then set their minds completely on God, He will make them into one heart and mind.

This is not as easy as it may sound. Before the presence of God is manifested, each elder must let go of arguments, pet doctrines, and other thoughts. The elder who is the most convinced about being right in any disagreement will be the very one who stops the manifesting presence of God. Before Jesus takes the reins, every person must "die" to his or her own way of looking at the problem. Often it requires several hours of seeking God before elders can forget the circumstances around themselves, clear out their minds, and truly worship Jesus. In addition, it is not easy to come together with another person, especially when both of them already have a disagreement. It is easier to run, to quit, to step down and not face the Lord with a brother or sister with whom there is a disagreement. To seek God with others takes a solid decision and a commitment.

God's ideal is that disagreements never develop. If elders regularly would seek God together, the devil never would get a foothold. When I was new in the ministry, I had weekly meetings with the leaders of our church during which we prayed for five minutes and then discussed church business for about two hours. Later I learned to reverse this order: we began by worshiping Jesus for about an hour, then we fellowshipped for an hour, and then we discovered that all our business could be dealt with during the last five minutes or so. First we sought God's unity, and then all else followed simply. And peace reigned.

A man or woman of God will be unafraid to seek God with others. I have seen that any time elders have been unwilling to enter into such a place of unity, it was because in their hearts they knew they were wrong and/or they were unwilling to give up their rebellious ways of thinking (which they were convinced were right); in other words, they were afraid to expose their thoughts and hearts to the presence of God. In reality, true men and women of God want their thoughts to be judged by God. They do not want sin in their own lives, and they realize they can make mistakes. Any elder (including an apostle) who refuses to seek God with others should be dismissed automatically from the position. The elder who rejects Jesus as Head of the Church is no longer a leader of God's church.

This is the safeguard for the Body of Christ. The apostle of a church has the final human authority over the other elders, but Jesus can overrule the apostle as long as all the elders are committed to seeking God together. Any elder with a rebellious heart can be identified and convicted by the presence of God. Any group of elders who earnestly seek God together will discover Jesus' ultimate authority. He will reign when we let Him.

The best situation occurs when the entire congregation comes together regularly and turns their thoughts upon God. That is when the presence of God and His molding power operate most powerfully. A Body that enters into God's presence consistently will not have divisions, strife, or confusion.

The manifesting presence of God is the power that allows all the gifts to work together. It is the oil that keeps the machine running. It is the binding power that overcomes disagreements among leaders. *Unity is the gift that God releases when everyone turns their thoughts completely onto Him.* The Holy Spirit, when His presence is manifested, releases Jesus to rule over His Church.

CHAPTER 28

THE GATHERING
AT THE
LAST OUTPOURING

Hand-in-hand with the last outpouring of God's Spirit and the Second Coming of Jesus will be the gathering together of the Church. God has promised to supernaturally draw His people into one:

> For thus says the Lord GOD, "Behold, I Myself will search for My sheep and seek them out. As a shepherd cares for his herd in the day when he is among his scattered sheep, so I will care for My sheep and will deliver them from all the places to which they were scattered on a cloudy and gloomy day....I will feed My flock and I will lead them to rest," declares the Lord God (Ezek. 34:11-15).

Many Christians see in this and similar Old Testament passages God's promise to draw together the Jewish people into one nation someday. But we can also see in these Scriptures a promise that our Lord one day will bring the New Testament people — His Church — into unity. We know this because Jesus declared Himself as the fulfillment of God's promise when He told us that He is the Good Shepherd who will call His own, and that we will "become one flock with one Shepherd" (John 10:16). Jesus prayed to the Father that we all would be one, and Paul wrote of a day when we would reach unity of the faith and also maturity (Eph. 4:13). One day, through Jesus Christ, God will bring all true Christians into agreement.

This does not negate the reality of future problems for the Church. The Bible tells us of great apostasy, tribulation, and persecution before Jesus returns. There will be many false prophets and deceived leaders. Masses of people will be led astray into beliefs that are abominable to God.

At the same time, the Bride of Christ will emerge, and the wineskin that forms will include all of the gifts of God. Jesus will send apostles to every city or region. Prophets and teachers will arise and move into their divinely appointed positions. All of the gifts will become evident, and they will function together in unity as one Body, with Jesus as the Head.

Just as the Charismatic movement crossed denominational lines, no walls will stop this coming move of God's Spirit. Some ministers who are already leaders in certain denominations will receive apostolic anointings. Others, who are unrecognized today by any organization, will be sent by God to do apostolic work. Prophets will arise from the upper class and from the poor. Teachers led by the Spirit will minister to whomever the Spirit directs, and never will be restricted by man-made barriers. Age will be no point of division either, as God chooses to anoint children as well as those approaching their century mark. Elders who have no education, training, or ministerial credentials will step out into powerful giftings. This coming move of God will cross every natural barrier that the world ever has known.

Those barriers also include sex. Some of the most anointed ministers will be women:

> "And it shall be in the last days," God says, "that I will pour forth of my Spirit upon all mankind; and your sons and your daughters shall prophesy...even upon my bondslaves, both men and women, I will in those days pour forth of my Spirit..." (Acts 2:17-18).

As the Spirit of God is allowed to move freely, He will work powerfully through women as well as men. As the early believers were amazed that God allowed the Gentiles to receive the Holy Spirit with tongues (Acts 10:44-48), many Christians are going to be amazed (and some may become angry) that God is greatly empowering women. God will distribute the gifts as He wills.

In this great outpouring of God's Spirit, there will be tremendous mergers of groups of believers. Several apostles, prophets, and teachers all will work together in divine unity within one city. If that city has one thousand pastors, each with a flock, those pastors will sense a bowing within their spirits to the apostolic anointings. Yokes of jealousy, doctrinal division, strife, and denominational separation will be broken. Pastors may continue to function as pastors, but they will be moved into their positions assigned by the Spirit. As God draws together His scattered sheep, pastors will bring their congregations under the headship of anointed apostles, prophets, and teachers, all under the headship of Jesus.

It is going to be glorious!

Some, however, will resist. As they do, they will find themselves with less and less of the zeal and energy of God to carry on in their ministries. Many leaders will find their congregations dwindling in size as believers yield to the Spirit and go to where the Spirit is moving. Some of the vacant positions in the pews of dead churches will be filled by those who are apostate, deceived, or hard-hearted. God will supernaturally separate the resistant ones from the sheep who hear His voice. Most of those who do not yield to this move of God will choose, instead, to stay with friends, family, and old acquaintances. Some will remain in dead churches because they want to hold on to their titles or positions. Thousands and thousands who never have been in the Church will feel a supernatural pull out of their homes and away from their present environments. It will be the fulfillment of Joel's prophecy concerning the last outpouring: "Multitudes, multitudes in the valley of decision!" (Joel 3:14). Every minister, layperson, and non-Christian will have to decide whether to follow the urging of the Spirit.

The leaders of this move will be persecuted. Just as those who first experienced the baptism in the Holy Spirit with tongues were mocked and ridiculed, so also will the forerunners of this next outpouring suffer rejection. If you think you were misunderstood when you first announced that you had received the gift of tongues or that you believed the spiritual gifts are still for today, just watch the eyebrows rise when you tell others (after God has instructed you to do so) that you have an apostolic, prophetic, or miracles anointing. As noted in Matthew 10:25, if even Jesus was rejected in His hometown when He made known His prophetic calling, how much more will His disciples be rejected! Some ministers will be shunned by their denominations. As hundreds were removed from their pulpits when they took a stand for the Spirit's gift of tongues, so also many will be expelled from comfortable positions when they admit to greater giftings. And yet, God will require His servants to step out boldly in their callings. But be encouraged, for those who suffer for His name's sake will receive great reward (Luke 6:22-23).

When will all this take place? I believe it already has started. This earth is presently being divided. The plumb line that Amos prophesied about has been dropped (Amos 7:8). Only two kingdoms will become evident: God's and Satan's. No kingdom divided against itself can stand, and therefore all walls within each domain must fall. One unified kingdom, ruled by the Antichrist, will emerge. At the same time, a glorious Church shall come forth. This is the hour for all about which the prophets spoke to be fulfilled.

Epilogue

EPILOGUE

THE CHURCH IN TRANSITION

After observing and experiencing the effects that the first three editions of this book have had on the Body of Christ, I want to clarify a few points and speak words of caution concerning the application of the principles taught. The following comments were born in victory and pain — mine and that of others.

The image of the future Church portrayed in this book is the ideal, the finished product, the place where God is taking us. Today, however, we are in transition. That means we are being carried along supernaturally toward an ultimate goal — but we are not there yet. Any Christian who looks around will not doubt that we have a long way to go. I point this out so that you will form a realistic view of our present position and of how much work we have ahead.

Neither you nor I can take the truths revealed in this book and force them into present reality through our own zeal and excitement. They should be recognized and understood, but as Jesus, the true Vine, reminds us, apart from Him we can do nothing (John 15:5). I can say this after personally failing many times in trying to implement these principles on my own. I also have watched earnest Christians attempt

171

to pattern their churches after the blueprint laid out here, and they have given up, discouraged and frustrated. Now that you have read this book, I encourage you not only to treasure these things in your heart, but to look to God for His direction in these matters.

What we need more than a new wineskin is new wine. We need the Holy Spirit, Who will empower us and give us wisdom. Without new wine the coming wineskin is empty and foolish. It is not leaders in the forms of apostles and prophets that we need. The missing piece right now is the hand of God. Seek Him — not a new structure.

At this very moment God is pouring out His Spirit afresh. The holy rain of grace is falling. We see it in the hunger now being quickened in the hearts of Christians everywhere. Believers are sensing that God has more for us than we presently are experiencing. The Holy Spirit's initial stirrings can be identified in the spirits of those now yearning to become all that God created them to be. Many, many believers are feeling that they were born for the coming hour. There is an awareness among Christians and non-Christians that God is about to do something awesome upon this earth. The Spirit is speaking.

I implore you: *Yield to the Holy Spirit.* He is the One Who is now at work in you. He has the plan to bring the Church into the fullness of Christ. Hundreds of steps lie between our present position and the glorious Bride to be revealed. Only God knows each step and the order in which He will lead us on them. No human being can make it all happen. We cannot set for ourselves a goal and then see it realized by our own efforts. It is the Spirit Who will lead us. Our responsibility is to follow Him. What God has begun in the Spirit He will finish in the Spirit.

Therefore, my counsel to you is this: Act on what God is telling you to do. Do not try to form "the complete wineskin" in your city. Just obey the Spirit today. Take the small steps that ultimately will lead to the fullness. The initial steps may seem small in light of God's all-encompassing plan, but they are significant. Perhaps God is simply asking you now to develop a deeper prayer life. Maybe He has been asking you to take one more step into your future anointing. Your traditional vocabulary concerning titles such as pastor and trustee may need to change. Perhaps there are thoughts in your mind that God is now trying to transform. Is it time you stopped viewing "church" as what happens Sunday mornings, and start "having church" in your home, over lunch, with your family, or whenever two or three Christians are with you? Perhaps the Spirit has been urging you to join a home fellowship. If you are an elder or a minister, the area needing immediate change may be in developing unity of mind with your co-laborers. Or perhaps God, at this moment, is interested in re-forming the wineskin of your heart with repentance and inner sanctification. Just do what God is telling you to do today.

As you and I and each member of the Body of Christ begin yielding to the Holy Spirit, we will find ourselves being molded supernaturally into His plan, into the victorious Church. We discussed this earlier, but it calls for our attention again. The prophets foretold of the end days, when every believer will be led individually and uniquely by the Spirit. As we each become submerged in the wind of the Spirit, we all will be blown into our God-ordained positions.

The Body of Christ is in transition. As I travel around and minister to churches, I observe various stages of our growth. Different groups are at different places. Some individuals are farther ahead than others. Of course, no one really can know another person's heart or fully understand what God is doing. But I'd like to offer my observations of what I see in the present Church.

The ministry that has been coming to the forefront and getting much attention lately is the prophetic ministry. Over the past few decades God has established the offices of pastor, evangelist, and teacher. Also, gifts of miracles and healing have been released. But at the time of this writing, God is causing the Body to accept prophets. Men and women in every part of the world are feeling a stirring in their hearts to become more bold and assertive. God has taken many of these people through training in preparation for the work coming upon us. At the same time, the entire Church is starting to open its doors for the prophetic office, desiring it to come forth both to clean up sin and to give clear direction. No one knows how long this period of prophetic restoration will last, but there is no doubt that we are in it right now.

It is important to recognize that not everyone who now has a "prophetic tendency" will enter into an office as a prophet. Many of them never will mature enough to become elders. Others never truly were called as prophets. In the last days God will cause a "spirit of prophecy" to fall upon the whole Church. The Church, therefore, will take on a prophetic bold, assertive nature for a period before the Second Coming. This is all in line with God's plan of raising an army, an uncompromising people of faith to stand against the coming darkness. The prophetic wave of the Spirit will prepare the way for the manifestation of the glorious Church in much the same way that John the Baptist preceded the coming of Jesus. I say this so that you will not confuse the *prophetic nature* falling upon Christians with the *office of prophet* being raised in the midst of the Body. Many Christians today think they are prophets, when in reality they merely are yielding to the Spirit of prophecy rising in their hearts. We must recognize the distinction.

Now here is a word to those who believe they will stand in the office of prophet: Pursue love. Labor for it. Treasure it and covet it for your life. Knowledge of the spiritual realm or of the future tends to make one arrogant (1 Cor. 8:1). When you see how far the present Church falls short, it is easy to get angry and even bitter. If you let related thoughts take root, you may be led into deception. Those who are not motivated by love can be nothing more than noisy gongs or clanging cymbals. Be a servant. Cry. Pray. Weep even more. Then be careful what you speak. As a fellow servant of our Lord Jesus Christ, I exhort you to let love be your highest aim.

All of those — not just prophets — who are moving into new anointings must follow those guidelines. It is too easy to get caught up in the excitement of our gifts and in what God is doing in these times. Although we have focused on all the various ministries in the Church, I fear that some may read these pages and become consumed in the concepts and ideas rather than in Jesus. We must keep the right perspective. Gifts and callings must not be the most important thing in anyone's life. There even will be times that we must lay down our own gifts and just be

God's humble servants. It is great to understand who we are and what God has placed us on this earth to do, but our foremost calling is simply to be His.

Let's now get back to the big overall picture of what God is doing in this hour. The prophets are coming forth, but before they are fully in their offices, God will pour out grace for the next stage. Then the end-time apostles will be positioned in the Body, and at last we will see the complete wineskin. First come the prophets and then the apostles.

This is not to deny the existence of apostles right now. There are already some leaders standing in the office of apostle. These are, indeed, apostles because God sent them to establish specific works. However, they are apostles to their individual churches or ministries.

There is coming an even greater anointing for the apostles for various cities. A new breed soon will take their positions across the land. Many of these future apostles already are sensing the call of God, but few, if any, have yet received the full anointing that God has for them. They are in the womb, soon to come forth for training and then for anointing. We can expect several apostles to arise in every larger city and many others to begin ministering outside our cities. The apostolic age is coming.

What will these apostles be like? They will walk with God. Their lives will be dedicated to prayer and to the ministry of the Word (Acts 6:4). They will be the ones who hold the authority over the local principalities. Through the lives of the modern apostles the grace of God will flow so that the complete wineskin can form.

How long will this restoration take? I don't know. But I am convinced that we are now in the beginning stages of the last great outpouring. Prophets are arising across the land, and they are speaking in various forms the message you just have read in this book. The Church is in transition. We can see it.

For years Christians have been praying for the last, mighty outpouring of God's Spirit. The time has come for our Lord to return. A powerful Church is being unveiled before our eyes; apostles and prophets even now are beginning to appear on the scene, and Christians are hungry to see God move in force. The stage is set. A new wineskin is taking shape. God is laying out the leather, drawing the pattern, and preparing to cut. The Spirit of God is beginning to pour out in greater measure than this world ever has seen.

Books That Will Change Your Life
by Harold R. Eberle

The Complete Wineskin (Fourth edition)

The Body of Christ is in a reformation. God is pouring out the Holy Spirit and our wineskins must be changed to handle the new wine. How are apostles, prophets, evangelists, pastors, and teachers going to rise up and work together? Where do small group meetings fit? Will the Church come together in unity? How does the anointing of God work and what is your role? This book puts into words what you have been sensing in your spirit. (Eberle's best seller, translated into many languages, distributed worldwide.)

God's Leaders for Tomorrow's World

(Revised/expanded edition) You sense a call to leadership in your life, but questions persist: "Why am I different? Is this pride? Others obey my instructions but do I truly know where to lead?" Through a new understanding of leadership dynamics, learn how to develop godly charisma. Confusion will melt into order when you see the God-ordained lines of authority. Fear of leadership will change to confidence as you learn to handle power struggles. Move into your "metron," that is, your God-given authority. You can be all God created you to be!

The Living Sword

"You shall know the truth and the truth shall set you free." So then why does Christian fight Christian over doctrinal issues that seem so clear to each side? Can both be right, or wrong? Learn how Jesus used the Scriptures in His day and then apply those principles to controversial issues currently facing us such as women in the ministry, divorce and remarriage, prosperity, predestination,.... What we need is the leading of the Holy Spirit on these subjects. This book will bring the Scriptures alive and set you free.

Two Become One

Releasing God's Power for Romance, Sexual Freedom and Blessings in Marriage

Learn how love works. Find out how to make God's law of binding forces work for you instead of against you. How does adultery take root from a seemingly blissful and innocent beginning? What happens to people when they divorce? The keys to a thrilling, passionate, and fulfilling marriage are yours if you want them, regardless of the circumstances.

Developing a Prosperous Soul
Vol. I: How to Overcome a Poverty Mind-set
Vol. II: How to Move into God's Financial Blessings

There are fundamental changes you can make in the way you think which will release God's blessings. This is a balanced look at God's promises with practical steps you can take to step into financial freedom. It is time for Christians to recapture the financial arena.

Spiritual Realities

(Now five volumes* of a seven volume series)

Here they are—the series explaining the spiritual world from a Christian perspective. In this series Harold R. Eberle deals with issues such as:

- What exists in the spiritual world
- How people access that realm
- Discerning things in the spirit
- Out-of-the-body experiences
- Interpretation of dreams
- What the dead are experiencing
- Angelic and demonic visitations
- Activities of witches, psychics and New Agers
- The Christian perspective of holistic medicine
- Spiritual impartations and influences between people
- Understanding supernatural phenomena from a Biblical perspective

Now you can have answers to the questions you always have wanted to ask about the supernatural world and spiritual phenomena.

Vol. I: The Spiritual World and How We Access It
Vol. II: The Breath of God in Us
Vol. III: Escaping Dualism

*Volumes IV & V Release Date: September 1998

*Vol. IV: Powers and Activities of Man's Spirit
*Vol. V: Spiritual Dynamics Between People

People Are Good, But Everyone Sins
A Fresh Look at the Nature of Man
Furthering the present reformation within the Church this book will cause a major paradigm shift in your mind. It will challenge fundamental beliefs, yet set Christians free and rejoicing. After reading this book you will look at life differently—more positively, more realistically, and with much more hope.

You Shall Receive Power
Moving Beyond Pentecostal & Charismatic Theology
God's Spirit will fill you in measures beyond what you are experiencing presently. This is not about Pentecostal or Charismatic blessings. There is something greater. It is for all Christians and it will build a bridge between those Christians who speak in tongues and those who do not. It is time for the whole Church to take a fresh look at the work of the Holy Spirit in our individual lives. This book will help you. It will challenge you, broaden your perspective, set you rejoicing, fill you with hope, and leave you longing for more of God.

Dear Pastors and Traveling Ministers,
Here is a manual to help pastors and traveling ministers relate and minister together effectively. Topics are addressed such as finances, authority, ethical concerns, scheduling,.... In addition to dealing with real-life situations, an appendix is included with very practical worksheets to offer traveling ministers and local pastors a means to communicate with each other. Pastors and traveling ministers can make their lives and work much easier simply by reading this manual.

For current prices or to place an order by phone, within the USA call: **1-800-308-5837** (MasterCard/Visa accepted)

Winepress Publishing
P.O. Box 10653, Yakima, WA 98909-1653, USA

E-mail: winepress@nwinfo.net
http: www.winepress.org

Some books available as an audiobook on cassette tapes.